Stories from Legend Singer

A Selection of Native American Legends as told by the Elders

Author
Jenny Ray

Available from Amazon.com and other retail outlets

Stories from Legend Singer

A Selection of Native American Legends as told by the Elders

By Jenny Ray
Original copyright © 2000
Second edition: copyright © 2014

*Illustrations By: Jenny Ray
Cover Art By: Jenny Ray and Kurt O'Donnell*

All rights reserved. No part of this book may be produced or transmitted in any form or by any means of electronic or mechanical, including photocopy, recording, or by any information retrieval system, or any other means of reproduction without the express written permission from the copyright owner and/or publisher, except in the case of brief quotations in articles and critical reviews where author and title are recognized by name.

Requests for reproduction permission can be mailed to:

Stone Medicine LLC
32708 N South Jackson Rd.
Elk, WA 99009

E-mail requests can be sent to:
jenny@SacredStoneMedicine.com

Published by Stone Medicine LLC

Introduction: Stories from Legend Singer

So who is Legend Singer? Well that was a name gifted to me at Castun (a Native American naming ceremony) by my father Chas Thompson. That name was chosen for me to recognize my desire to learn the legends and stories told by my Native mentors. To add confusion to the whole 'name' issue, my birth certificate name is Virginia Rae, my nick name is Jenny Ray which is how all artwork, and writings are signed by me. The newest name I received at Castun in 2000 is Ska Matho Pejuta Winan (White Bear Medicine Woman). So now that you know all my A.K.A.'s, you can just call me Jenny!

This book is a work of fiction. The stories and legends written in this book are recorded from my memory, with a few adlibs here and there to fill them in. When the original storyteller can be identified a brief introduction is offered.

This book has not received nor implies that any permission or endorsement from any Native American tribe exists. These stories were taught to me by individuals who, in most cases, have passed on. They were repeating stories they had heard from long ago forgotten sources or by those who wished to remain anonymous or they might have been the creator of the story.

This book is for your enjoyment and to stimulate your imagination to create stories for the next generation. Many children in our modern world live at the hectic pace of their parent's over-scheduled lives. If you can take a few minutes now and then to tell a child a story, or read them one, you will find your heart opens to the magic of a youthful imagination.

Take a journey with a five year old and remember the excitement and mystery that flows through every breath. Forget about the daily stress of working, finances, politics, or relationships. Look at the bright spirit that shines from those eager eyes and fall in love with life again. The constant pressures to achieve, gain, succeed and prosper, have robbed some of us of the most precious gifts in life, innocence and imagination.

Nurturing the next generation with the emotional and spiritual food of parental attention, began to disappear for many or our families, as the world grew more complex, over the past few decades. Some of us were so busy trying to feed the little bodies of our children that we rarely took time to feed their hearts and minds with the true love we held for them. As I age, I see the neglected children of my youth become adults who are trying to bridge that gap. They are amazing and wonderful parents and even grandparents now, in spite of me, not because of me.

I love my children with all my heart and to this day have not found a way to express it in terms that are adequate. I hope every parent that understands that feeling can make a choice to bring storytelling back to their world. Yes, it is a gift to live in this comfortable electronic age, but the price may be too high in retrospect for some of us. That television program, movie, video game or other babysitter has no compassion for your child. The human day-care center, pre-school, grade school, club, sports team, artistic education, extracurricular activity, or even Sunday school cannot replace your lap and a gentle embrace during story-time for a child.

Slow down, sit quietly, listen to their thoughts, share stories, and thank Creator for the wisdom to not miss this moment.

If you have little ones in your life and the chance to 'get it right', include storytelling in your nurturing and you will have an old age filled with joyful memories rather than regrets.

Dedication

I dedicate this book to my children who have not heard enough good stories.

To my grandchildren and great-grandchildren who I hope will hear many!

These stories are dedicated to the child within each of us who can still learn from the wisdom of imagination.

Today's actions become tomorrow's stories and in a few generations, they are the legends. We are living the legends of our children's children.

To my perfect and wonderful Children, Grandchildren and Great-grandchildren, I hope you know how very much you are loved.

Create your own legends by living your best lives.

Acknowledgments

How can I thank my ancestors? They are the ones who have passed down these stories and legends so that we may know where our traditions come from. I believe I can thank them best by passing them on. Each storyteller has a way of holding the content of the message and addressing it in the way they heard it. Every storyteller will speak in their own vernacular, influenced by their heritage, back ground and current society, molded by their environment, education, philosophies, and spiritual beliefs. I have tried to tell these stories and legends just as I heard them, acknowledging those influences in my own life.

A dear and longtime friend from the Nez Perce tribe, Earl "Tazz" Conner, taught me the stories from the Nez Perce people. When I wrote the words of those legends, I heard them in his voice and even found myself writing in his particular speech pattern at times. It was a wonderful experience for me to hear him, in my mind, as he told these great stories. I only wish you could have sat around the same campfire and seen his smile and heard his laugh. He has 'Crossed the River" now and we all miss him.

When I heard legends from Bird Woman, I could hardly wait to repeat them. She had a way of using her wonderful voice to create the sounds of the animals and made us all want to join her in their songs. Her generosity of knowledge and her desire to 'make it that way' has helped me to honor the legends of all Nations. She was a difficult teacher at times with her snappish ways and that constant preening of every detail. I felt as if her real name could have been 'Chicken Woman' at times, as her peck, peck, pecking at me to 'make it like that' was so frustrating to me as her young student. That frustration of my youth has turned to respect and appreciation in my elder years, as I see the gift of preservation in her ways. The stories she has allowed me to share with the non-Native community are a treasure that she feared were over-looked by the dominant society.

I share her wisdom and words with great humility now as I realize the gift was offered to one who could not appreciate the depth of the lessons or the gift of 'tradition' at the time. She is one of my most valued mentors. And although her years were few and her life un-remarkable according to the yard stick of success, I am blessed to share a few of her words with you in this little book.

Another fine storyteller who had a huge influence on me, and these writings, is my father, Charles (Chas/Chuck) Thompson. Through his wit and humor, I have learned a great deal about my Indian heritage. He loved to tell of his days as a youth in Torrington, Wyoming, The Dakotas, and Montana. As he shared his life experience, he helped to weave another generation of storytellers into the fabric of our people. Thank you Dad, for passing on the gift of storytelling, which I enjoy so much!

Dad liked to hear his own voice and would often record himself telling stories or composing his philosophies as he drove down the road. With his tape recorder clicking off the miles he filled his time with his own thoughts and unwittingly (or not) preserved a volume of stories that I treasure. One afternoon he sat in his vendor booth at an Idaho show, telling my sister Nancy and me about the Horse Drum Stick legend. It is a day I recall with many smiles as I remember him starting and stopping the tape recorder to be sure he had all of our 'linage' spoken correctly. Although he continuously mixed up the Oglala and the Dakota, I found records of both in our heritage with the prominent blood lines going back to the Santee People. The tape has long since been destroyed, but the memory lives on.

He liked to say he was a 'jack-of-all-trades and good-at-none'. And in his case that was a fact. He worked several different trades in his lifetime. From a ranch hand, cowboy, carpenter, building inspector, politician, auctioneer, business owner (none of much success) and all round character he worked hard and for the most part, loved life. He loved his kids and tried to build relationships with the adults we became, after struggling to be present during our childhoods. There are five of us altogether from two different moms, so he was in and out of our lives at times, but always ready to fill the void with his stories. I am grateful some of them can now be shared with others through these written words.

I thank my mom (born ~ Othela Jean Towell) Jean Carper and all our family of storytellers. Some of those stories have been written in poetry, others were sang in songs and the best ones were at Grandpas' knee, where we all listened like hungry birds. Mom, you are so good at keeping us connected and helping the legends of our family continue. Just today on the phone, you gave me another story from our Cherokee Grandma Turner's life, which adds to the legends we hold sacred as a family.

My Grandpa Towell was a master storyteller with a gentle voice and an easy laugh. He loved to be with his grandchildren, especially when they were pre-school age and encourage them to spin a yarn. He would ask the question 'then what happened...' over and over as you tried to share an experience with him. And of course the child was honor bound to keep talking, so the story would grow and grow until the end was achieved when Grandpa could hold back the laughter no longer and would scoop you up in his arms with a big hug and say something like 'what a great story'! He never accused you of lying or making up some tale. He acted as if your imagination run wild was a good thing! And so it was. Thank you Grandpa, for helping me fall in love with stories and legends!

The legends gathered for this book are from my Native American family, while the ones from my Irish family will wait for another 'story-time'.

I want to thank my best computer geek, best partner and best of all, my husband, Kurt O'Donnell. Thank you for always being there when I need your advice, wisdom, and reassurance. The hours of assistance you have offered during the creation of this book are innumerable. I have appreciated your patience as I stumble along with the computer. I am grateful for the way you have ignored the 'truck driver' language that I speak at this silly machine. You just ignored my not too lovely way to vent those 'computer illiterate' frustrations, which could have stifled this project. Thanks for the assistance, space, and time to move through this process.

Not many people can say they have a mother-in-law that they love, but I do. I am one of the lucky ones who have in-laws that are awesome, so a big thank-you to Brian and Betty O'Donnell. The support on so many fronts is greatly appreciated. I would not have the confidence to put these stories out for the world to see if you did not give them a read over first and encourage me to share them. About the time I think I cannot do something you become the cheerleader I need and I move forward to try and live up to your enthusiasm!

Finally to my best friend, best editor and tireless Stone Walker buddy, Janelle Lakman, thank you! Your hours of editing and advice have helped these stories come into print. Your efforts make all this possible. Your time and energy is so precious to me and I understand how much I have asked of you at times. I am not sure I could ever be such a generous and supportive friend. I am amazed at how often you say 'let me know what I can do…' and you really mean it!

The Go-Fund-Me project opened the door for folks to make a contribution to the self-publishing efforts that have put this book in print…and I am overwhelmed by your generosity…I pray each of you is blessed with your heart's desire (or with what is good for you…) I am grateful to all of you named and un-named who have made this book possible!

Contents

Forward 3

Sacred Prayer Fan 11

Talking Feather 21

Legend of the Dream Catcher 27

Chipmunk, Snake and Fire 39

Nez Perce Sweat Lodge 45

A Creation Story 51

Hollow Bone Legend 95

Selfish Chief 119

White Buffalo Calf Woman 139

Forward

The Power of Legends

Many traditional stories and legends from the Native American community have been lost, for lack of interested ears. Some folks are finding it is time to revive some of these traditional stories. We need to glean from them the lessons they so artfully taught. The personal and moral values these ancient ones expressed in stories and legends, could serve modern human-kind with the missing ingredients necessary for peace.

We all understand that history is recorded by the conquerors and that they justify the victory by belittling the conquered. But I still have hope, that the real Americans, the Native and First Nation People of North and South America, will one day be honored with the respect they deserve. It is time that as a Nation we Americans will begin to listen and learn from them, about a true relationship with Mother Earth.

We have a collective consciousness in America that will not allow us to be the true leaders of the free world until we find a way to recognize the truth of our history. We must stop treating 99% of our citizens as slave labor to serve the 1% of wealth and means. As we challenge the world to be better stewards of the environment and to protect human rights, we as a Nation fall short of the very expectations we place on others.

We know in our hearts that many wrongs were, and still are, heaped on the people of this land. We have built our great cities on the bones of an indigenous people who could not withstand the sheer numbers of the invaders. Of course this must have been in the grand plan of our Creator the Great Mystery, the one and only God of all peoples, but finding our way to true peace requires us to acknowledge the sins of our fathers and to stop procreating them for the future.

The heaviness of knowing our ancestors suffered

unfairly at the hands of the white settlers is only one part of the story. As a mixed blood I carry sadness for my Irish ancestors as well, who traveled across the great waters, to avoid the famine that covered their land. Leaving behind family and possession to venture to the 'New World' in the hopes of finding a life for themselves and their descendants, must have taken every ounce of bravery these good people could find.

We know now that the great potato famine was caused by poor farming skills and it nearly cost a wonderful people their very existence.

We are facing a worldwide environmental crisis. Possibly not the first for this planet, but one that will affect our future generations in ways only imagined. I think of the commercial a few years back with the old Indian man looking sadly at trash along a highway, with the single tear dripping down his face and am reminded that many people believe the Natives have a relationship with Mother Earth. That version of our imagined love for Mother Earth should be emulated by all. In some ways that picture of the native relationship with our earth is true, but a drive through most reservations will show you how difficult it is to blend poverty and a spiritual relationship with the land.

Old, dead, car bodies litter the land on reservations, because it is cheaper to buy another old car than it is to haul off the one that died. Besides that old car is a pretty good closet if you do not have any storage space and do not dare throw anything away! The sad truth is that many Native American families struggle to survive in our modern world and the wisdom of their traditions are held in broken hearts.

As I bring some of the stories from our elders to the world, I pray that a blessing can come to those who live on the reservation lands near our ancestor's bones. When a voice from the past speaks through the written word, it often is louder than the one spoken in life, to deaf ears. I hope by sharing some of these words I am supporting the wisdom keepers of Turtle Island. Every guru form every nation is heard by this melting pot we call the United States of America, while the voice of our own indigenous ancestors is often hidden under the dominant societies' veil of secrets.

It is time for the hidden truth of our history to be revealed. Many generations have suffered behind closed doors and drawn curtains. A few have ventured forth to enlighten the masses about the hardships of reservation life, boarding school scandals, church dominance, and government oppression. Yet rarely has a light been cast on the depth of this on-going challenge for our indigenous brothers and sisters.

While the struggles of our African American cousins have continued, many Native Americans wonder when the world will also see them. While the black folks struggled with sitting in the back of the bus, we simply wanted to get *on* the bus. While signs marked 'black' and 'white' drinking fountains, the Indian was forced to drink from the garden hose, dog dish or horse trough.

While the government demanded proof of blood purity from an individual who might have one drop of black blood, in order to be eligible to vote, work at certain jobs, attend various education facilities and receive medical treatment at the white man's care facilities, it was simultaneously demanding proof of blood percentages for Native heritage. The years of 'assimilation' practices aimed at ridding the nation of Indians had diluted blood lines in hopes of wiping out the race entirely.

The offer of forty acers and a mule for any white man who married an Indian woman led to horrendous abductions and child brides in one of the worst human tariffing records in world history. Oh that's right there is no official record of this! The 'Indian problem' as seen by Washington was to be dealt with on many fronts. One of the first records of germ warfare happened on American soil. It was delivered by gifting small pox, chicken pox and measles infected blankets to the tribes. Wiping out hundreds of people and nearly destroying various tribes. Oh yes, there is no history books on this in my child's school.

Unfortunately we humans in our small minded ways often pick up the traits of our abusers and carry them forward. Now as Black people discriminate amongst themselves over the color of their skin, with light being best and dark being worst. Native American tribes also inflict damage by judging people with mixed blood as not 'red' enough. If the individual resembles their white ancestors more than the Native ones, it is possible they do not 'look' Indian and can be shunned. If the paperwork of enrollment cannot be traced through the governments, error ridden, Dawes Rolls it is possible your entire family could be left off the tribal enrollment documents and your rights as a Native American can be withheld.

Indian hiring at Indian owned businesses might not apply to your child of mixed race even if you are a member of the tribe because their percentage of blood has fallen below the acceptable arbitrary quantity required by the government. You could find yourself, in contemporary Indian life struggling to prove your birth linage because the paperwork is not there to support your beliefs in your heritage.

It was illegal for us to offer traditional ceremonies during my young years, until then president, Jimmy Carter took up the native cause: *American Indian Religious Freedom Statement on Signing S.J. Res. 102 into Law. August 12, 1978,*
Public Papers of the Presidents ~ Jimmy Carter
I have signed into law S.J. Res. 102, the American Indian Religious Freedom Act of 1978. This legislation sets forth the policy of the United States to protect and preserve the inherent right of American Indian, Eskimo, Aleut, and Native Hawaiian people to 'believe, express, and exercise their traditional religions. In addition, it calls for a year's

evaluation of the Federal agencies' policies and procedures as they affect the religious rights and cultural integrity of Native Americans.

It is a fundamental right of every American, as guaranteed by the first amendment of the Constitution, to worship as he or she pleases. This act is in no way intended to alter that guarantee or override existing laws, but is designed to prevent Government actions that would violate these constitutional protections. In the past, Government agencies and departments have on occasion denied Native Americans access to particular sites and interfered with religious practices and customs where such use conflicted with Federal regulations. In many instances, the Federal officials responsible for the enforcement of these regulations were unaware of the nature of traditional native religious practices and, consequently, of the degree to which their agencies interfered with such practices.

This legislation seeks to remedy this situation."

Many changes have happened in my lifetime to ease some of the prejudice and injustice that plague our fellow Americans. Finally, Thank God, our nation's media realizes they should not say the 'n' word. Yet an equally offensive racial epitaph directed at Native Americans, can be used to title multimillion dollar sports teams.

In this world where the romantic Hollywood version of the American Indian is fully embraced, we ignore the sovereignty of the nations threatened by an oil pipeline.

Most of those Hollywood Indian roles were filled by white actors in make-up or by Mexicans from our southern relative's tribes. That was because; Indians were not allowed to work on the set. We understand that 'black face' is an outrage for the stage, but the 'westerns', movies made by John Wayne and Roy Rodgers are filled with non-Indian people playing the roles of Native Americans. And always the Indian was the supporting character, think Tonto', or the heathens filled with war whoops and tomahawks slaughtering innocent white settlers. These old westerns are still played on the classic movie channels.

Strides have been made in the last few decades, but the distance to cover will require giant leaps and bounds, to bring our indigenous peoples of North and South America to an equal playing field. While we bicker over gender rights, gun rights, and other assumed 'rights, we ignore human rights. We claim to have evolved and yet hide from our own foolish failures.

We must learn how to respect and accept the differences in each other before we can enjoy our similarities. We have to see beyond the limitations of that small human, judgment eye, that traps us in old paradigms of prejudice, hatred, and fear. True peace comes from more than tolerance; it comes from the righteous acceptance of our differences. It comes from the joyful embrace of our uniqueness.

If we *wish* to change the world, we have to do more than *wish* it. We must make a commitment to leave the next generation with more bounty, than we took for ourselves. New Age philosophy is urging us to return to Mother Earth, live a spirit filled life, be a 'beacon of hope', and let the 'change begin with me'. That is all grate and wonderful, but absolutely not new news.

If you listen between the lines of these ancient legends and stories you will hear the same information. We have been speaking these truths for generations and even though we might string the words together a bit differently, the message has never changed.

If we are to be a productive society that can withstand the ages and not disappear ourselves like the ancient ones of Egyptian pyramids, Rome, Aztec and Inca empires, then we must actually heed the lessons preserved in our words.

For thousands of years, storytelling served most cultures as a means of preserving history and tradition, passing on spiritual guidance, and shaping acceptable values, integrity, and human behaviors. We think we are living in such difficult times with complicated circumstances, so it is just too simple to believe that basic truths of love, honor, and respect can change the world. That is not true. We are only more arrogant than the ones who came before us. While we look for the difficult solutions to our complex problems, the simple truth still holds our answers.

The days prior to the industrial revolution were very difficult for the people living on the land. People of all nations were struggling for territory and survival. Each day was filled with searching for food and often shelter just to survive. One blessing of that time was a close community where family was truly the center of life. Long winter evenings gave time for quiet contemplation and reflection. These were the times children gathered at the feet of elders, around the fire and asked for stories.

If we want to apply the beautiful writings of Maya Angelo or the Dali Lama and the literally hundreds of writers before and since them, we can look to the scriptures, ancient texts and legends they are based on, to find the thread of truth that runs through them all. We could choose to live the stories we tell our children and become the adults who put away the childish things.

The legends from Native Americans, First Nation People, Aboriginals, and indigenous Natives worldwide carry the same message. We need to consider the kind of world we could create by heeding the lessons wrapped in the words of our ancestors.

We must begin to apply these truths as members of the human race and stop playing the game of egocentric, genetic superiority. When we hear our politicians, and other leaders we choose, speak disrespectfully of one another, and lie for the sake of gathering a vote, we know that our society is driving down that well-traveled road of self-destruction. We recognize that rotten fruit, of disrespect and dishonorable words, yet we feast on this withering tree as if it holds nourishment for the soul.

When we truly choose to meet the expectations of our Creator, whatever you choose to believe that is, by following the guidelines set forth for acceptable human behavior, we just might discover 'world peace' is more than a platitude offered by beauty queen contestants.

I hope you enjoy this gathering of stories and recognize many of the values they offer, as the ones we should live by. Whatever your spiritual beliefs I hope you can see the truths preserved in these legends as the ones necessary for peace. In our modern age we often think of stories as a simple form of entertainment, but more commonly, they are educational in nature as well as divinely inspired.

If you choose not to look deeper within for spiritual or cultural enlightenment, I hope you will at least enjoy the journey of imagination these legends offer. The power of legends can be transformative or simply entertaining. Even in our modern life, who does not enjoy the re-telling of a treasured story?

Sacred Prayer Fan

This legend was shared by Bird Woman who taught me how to make Prayer Fans. At the time I was a divorced single mom and a struggling artist who needed to supplement my income, so she suggested I 'craft' some traditional Native Replicas. I had been studying the traditions of several tribes for many years and thought I had fair understanding about Native spiritual beliefs. My father had focused on sharing Sioux traditions and my friend Tazz had taught me about many Nez Perce ceremonies. I never knew for sure what Bird Woman's tribe of enrolment was. She had lived on the Umatilla reservation near Pendleton, Oregon as a child. Her youth was spent on the Grande Ronde along the Oregon coast and she spoke of the Rose Bud and Pine Ridge reservations in South Dakota. Never one to share much of her personal story she was an individual who taught the most profound ceremonial traditions I have ever learned. She died in the late 1990's and I am sorry to say, I never knew who her people were.

I thought I was only going to learn how to glue some feathers to a stick and make a couple dollars. But I should have known better, Bird Woman had a different plan!

She started by teaching me the value of making a traditional item and how to own a sacred item. I was not sure I even believed in a sacred item at that time in my life. She taught me the difference between honoring and caring for an item used in prayer and ceremony, rather than worshiping an item. She gave me her perspective on how all of us have rituals and traditions and even sacred items.

Bird Woman was always a tough old bird and she did not pull any punches in her teaching style. She would lead me down the path of self-discovery and allow me to convince myself of her wisdom. She asked so many questions that you felt she never told you anything. It was her most powerful method of enlightenment. Her constant pecking was irritating and awkward to deal with, but it certainly made you think deeper than you had planned.

When she asked me about my rituals and ceremonies, I admitted that I was not practicing any at that time. She huffed out a scoff and said, "you lie." That was her style, but I was still shocked by her blunt words. She said she could prove it and had me tell her about my morning routine. I explain that I had a set pattern of waking to a cup of coffee and a smoke before I even brushed my teeth and how next the bathroom visit was my time for shower, hair fixing, and make-up before work. Then she asked me to shake up my 'ritual' and do it different for the next 7 days.

What the heck this had to do with making a craft item was beyond me, but if I was to learn from her, I had to do it her way. The next day found me out the door to work with less coffee than required and my hair a mess. I called and told her 'I got it', but she just said 'good see you in six more days', and hung up. She had me do this shaking up of my ritual, for an entire week! It was awkward and uncomfortable and I could not wait to return to my natural rhythm. By the third day I had a written list of what needed to be done every morning. This was so I would not forget something as I mixed it up to please Bird Woman. Boy she was a pain! I could not just move mindlessly through the 'ritual' of my morning without a set routine and even with the written list it was uncomfortable.

Bird Woman explained how it is human nature to create ritual, ceremony, pattern, repetition, and reproducible systems. We can tie that to our spiritual beliefs or we can just say it is habit, but without 'ritual' we are not in balance. Then she started asking 'why' to everything I did in my morning routine. Why the coffee and smoke first? Why the teeth brushing next, why, why, why! She told me if I was going to make prayer fans I better have spiritual rituals or I would forget to pray and that would make the fans worthless. It was during this week that my spiritual practice of morning prayers was established in my heart and not just my head. But I still was not convinced about 'sacred items'.

One day she tapped an un-tanned, impression on my finger where my wedding band had been for worn years. "What's that?" She knew what it was. But by the time I finished explaining to her how I had never taken it off in all those years, until the marriage was over, I had also told her it had been a sacred item. Placed during a ritual, with a vow made to honor what it stood for. Yes I understood I did not worship the item, but it was sacred to me none the less.

This gave her permission to tell me the reasons behind everything I needed to know before I could start making a prayer fan. Why would I want Wild Turkey feathers to represent Eagle feathers? Here it was week two and I had not touched a feather yet! She taught me the 'medicine' (energy or message that they stood for) of each bird that I might harvest feathers from. She taught me about the deer before I could purchase any leather. She taught me about the willow, cedar, and pine tree before I could choose a branch for the wooden handle.

The third week I was sure we would start making this

beautiful item that I was now beginning to crave. But instead, that was the week this legend first spoke to me. I had heard it from her voice many times before, but it never impacted me like that day. The next week we began gathering the materials for my first fan, and it changed my life.

I must admit that first prayer fan was never sold. It became a 'sacred item' to me. I still have parts of it incorporated into the fan I use today. Yes I learned about so much more than a craft item. As I share this legend I hope I do justice to her words. And I hope you learn between the lines some of the valuable lessons she taught me. Not that I can always apply them, but I am better for having tried.

At the beginning of time, before someone put it in the clock box, Turtle Island rose up from the bottom of the sea. It became our home. The people could send prayers to Wakhan Tunkasila (Sacred Grandfather) on the wings of Eagle, whose name is Wambli. This was such a long time ago, even before the gift of Chanupa (the pipe). It was so long ago no one can remember unless we tell this story.

When the people's prayers became too many for

Wambli to carry alone, he called to his brother, Spotted Eagle, for a council.

"Great Mystery, Creator of us all has given me a very important job to do and I need your help," said Eagle.

"What is this job?" asked Spotted Eagle.

"To carry the prayers of the people into the great beyond, all the way to Creators ears," answered Eagle.

"With your mighty wings and strong muscles you should need no help with this, my brother," said Spotted Eagle.

"At first this was true, but now there are more people than Eagles and we cannot get all the prayers to Creator fast enough. The people now seem to have more to be grateful for so they are praying more," said Wambli.

"Well that is all good news, for I am sure Wakhan Tunkasila has planned it all this way. What help can I give you?" asked Spotted Eagle.

"Take as many prayers to Creator as you can carry and have all our spotted brothers do the same" said Wambli.

"With pride and honor I accept this duty my brother" said Spotted Eagle.

Things went well for many generations. Then a time of sadness and war came to Mother Earth. There were tribes fighting amongst themselves. Many people did ceremony and made prayers. The smudge fires and prayers being offered began to grow to such a large number that all Eagles and all Spotted Eagles could not carry them to Creator.

Grandfather Wambli called for a council with all the Winged Ones. They came from all over Turtle Island to hear the words of Grandfather Wambli.

He explained the trouble. "The ceremonies and offerings of the two-legged (people) are becoming too many for the Eagle family to carry."

"We must gather the prayers from the lips of the Two Legged and carry them to the highest places for Creator's ears. Then when Creator speaks the answer, we must bundle the prayer answers and carry them back to the correct heart" said Grandfather Wambli.

Grandfather Wambli hung his head and said "I fear that a time is coming when the people will offer many more prayers to Creator because of a great danger. We cannot let them pray to Wind for he cannot carry the words without them being tumbled around. We cannot ask Sister Moon or Brother Sun as they have important jobs keeping day and night alive with their light. This takes all their power and we cannot leave these Two Leggeds in darkness. We cannot ask mighty Thunder Beings to carry the people's prayers for the prayers could not be heard over their mighty voice and Lightning might burn them up."

Grandfather Wambli continued, "Cloud beings are busy bringing rain, snow and shade so they have no time to carry prayers. The Star Tribe is doing a great job of keeping order in the skies by shining all night and hiding all day. This is a Winged One's duty. This duty has been ours from the beginning of time. Now we must find ways to solve this problem so not one word or thought of the People is lost. How can we work together to solve this problem?" he asked

Some thought mighty Raven could help, but he and his Hawk cousins were so busy bringing messages and guidance from Creator to the people that they had even asked for help. They explained how Creator wanted to teach the people how to be better servants to each other, so he would tell Hawk and Raven many important things. Then Raven told the Great Mystery's lessons to many Four Legged and small Winged Ones, who could carry them to the Two Legged people.

Raven knew how to give many lessons to the Creepy Crawlers, and even to the Swimming Ones and the many Rooted Ones growing from Mother Earth. All these relations were giving the People education from Creator. Raven was given more lessons each day by Creator, to disperse to the many helpers Creator had made. They were busy trying to get the Two Legged to listen to the lessons offered by Creator through all His creation. That was plenty for him and his brothers to do. They could not assist Wambli.

Many thought they should ask Small Eagle (red tailed hawk) for help, but he already had the job of bring together the people and the spirit world. He could visit with the people in many ways. Small Eagle even worked at night in the dream world and often in visions he would bring good medicines from others in the animal world to teach the people important lessons.

Brother Owl was busy warning of dangers. He was feared and dreaded by some of the Two Legged People, not because he was harmful, but because he was warning of some bad thing that could happen. He was protecting the people by helping them to know when they would need to prepare for trouble. Owl was sharing wisdoms in the dream time and as the silent night flyer he was able to help the people put the prayer answers into action.

Many of the other large and powerful Winged Ones had given up their ability to fly fast and sore high. Ones like Land Eagle, who is called Turkey, had chosen to provide food for the people with their bodies so they now stayed closer to the land so the people could hunt them easier. They knew the body must be well fed before the spirit can be nourished.

Many of the smaller Winged Ones who spent their lives singing happy songs and planting seeds, volunteered to help. But they were just too small to fly so high and the people needed them to do their own jobs. The many lessons they each taught and the good medicines they brought were very important to the balance and harmony of the people and all the relations. Every small Winged One knew where to live and what to plant and when to harvest and where to go in winter. They were guides for the people on the long journey to safe Winter-grounds and they helped bring them home to the Spring-lands of abundance.

After days of talking and hours of praying, old Grandfather Wambli said, "I am old and my feathers are worn, you can see by the white color of my head that much time has passed for me. I am nearly finished here but I cannot leave until I know the Two Legged People can send their prayers and sacred herb smoke up to Creator on feathers from our mighty Winged Ones."

Sadly he lifted one of his wings sky-ward.

He looked at the battered old wing and realized it could use some repair, but he was too tired.

"If I could just lay this set of feathers aside and only pick them up when I needed to carry prayers, they might stay in better shape" he mumbled to himself.

As he took inventory of his feathers he began to realize that even with just a few feathers in one small bunch he could still move the air and send prayers to Creator.

"I wish I could just give all the People a few of my feathers to wave sky-ward and send prayers to The Great Mystery," he thought out loud. At that very moment he felt a warm glow of Creator's love flood over him and he knew this was the plan. Suddenly his eyes grew bright and he flapped his wings and screeched out for attention from the gathering.

"Wakhan Tunkasila has just given me an answer to our problem," yelled Grandfather Wambli.

"Tell us quickly!" They called out.

"When I go to Mother Earth tonight I will lay down my body in the long sleep for 'Crossing the River of Life' and join our ancestors. Before I go, I will make one last gift to the people" he spoke humbly.

Some thought the old one was not thinking straight in his mind and cocked their heads at each other. They had seen him mumbling to himself and even ignoring his grand appearance. But this kind of talk was not normal for Wambli.

"Listen my brothers and sisters and all my cousins, I will go in a dream to the Shamans in every village across

Mother Earth. I will show them how to use a few feathers to make a Sacred Fan. They will be able to teach all in the tribe how to create these fans and before long they will be able to send the prayer smoke to Creator with only a bit of help from us. We can soar above the lands on high winds and gather the prayers from these high places then carry them but a short way to Wakhan Tunkasila" Wambli spoke with dignity.

"We will all give our gifts to the people. Now when you drop a feather it will be gathered by the people and handled with honor. They will know you left this gift for them and they will thank our Creator for you." Wambli was standing tall and strong as he spoke these words.

All the Winged Ones thought about Grandfather Wambli's words and knew that he had just been honored by the Great Mystery. To think that they could leave a few feathers here and there for the people to find and in this way give their medicine and teach the lessons was indeed a magical thing.

That very night Wambli joined Great Owl and went from dream to dream in all lodges, of all tribes. He let them see how to honorably gather feathers. He taught them the thanksgiving prayer. He showed them how to dress these sacred feathers and told them to call these beautiful sacred items 'Prayer Fan'. He knew that these lessons would be passed down in the traditional way to all the generations through stories and songs.

Now that his work was finally finished he could Cross the Great River and rest. He knew he had done a good thing and that the people would never worry about prayers being lost. Many generations have sent prayers to Wakhan Tunkasila with these fans and we are honored to use our best creative energies to continue in tradition by making them still.

All feathers from all the Winged Ones are special gifts. They are used by the People to decorate outfits and lodges and to place in long black hair. They are made into beautiful gifts for honoring each other. The leaders, Shamans, Medicine Men and Medicine Women as well as the Chiefs of each tribe are given many of Eagle's feathers for their powerful staffs and dance sticks and out-fits. Eagle feathers sometimes fly above the tipi on tall lodge poles to protect the family inside.

Even though all feathers are honored the greatest is Eagle. Great Wambli is honored for his gift to the People and his feathers have many sacred ceremonies just for them. Eagle is the one chosen by Creator for all the people to celebrate.

Talking Feather

This legend was told many times in a variety of ways by my father (Chas~ to his Native friends, Chuck~ to his white friends) Thompson. He would carry it on for an hour if a child was enthralled, or could get the message across in a few moments if the legend just needed to make a point for an adult. His favorite way to tell stories was with lots of sound effects, funny faces, hand gestures, and accents. He used to tell every off-color Irish joke he heard, using his favorite Irish brogue. In this legend, each sound was pitch-perfect to the real bird!

When the warm summer sun has rested on the berry vines long enough, the colors will call to our people and say, "Here we are for picking and eating."

This call came to the young mothers in our village one day long, long ago. So they took their baskets and went to gather the fruit. When the old Grandmother's legs have lost the fast walk and sure foot of the doe, they are not much help on the gathering trips. The young people honor their Grandmothers by giving them an important duty on these days. The youngest of the children, who are our future, are left in the care of these old ones.

We believe that the little ones have many dreams and visions to collect before they can grow in the wisdoms of their people. We try to give them a bit of sleep in the warmth of a darkened lodge before Sun has traveled his full path each day. Now let me tell you what happened on one of these days.

Crow and Magpie, two of our noise-making winged cousins, were having a terrible argument outside the lodge of the sleeping children.

"Caaaw-caaaw" screamed Crow.

"Kaaack- Kack- Kack" yelled Magpie.

They were both speaking at once and could not even hear each other's point of view, on the subject of which branch belonged to which bird.

At first, one of the Grandmothers asked Creator to quiet the voices outside. This was easier on her old bones than going out to take care of it herself. But Creator let the Grandmother know that it was her job to go out and quiet these birds. You see, Wakhan Tunkasila knew that a great gift was coming to the people and he wanted the youngest Grandmother to help carry out his plan.

She was not really young at all, but was not as old as some of the grandmothers that day. This grandmother's name was Bird Song. She was told in her 'knowing place', to go out and send these noisy winged cousins away. She slowly walked to the tree where the dispute was getting louder by the minute.

She called out in her small old woman voice, "Hey you! Crow, take that fussing away from this sleeping lodge."

Crow was not listening; he was talking, so he never heard the Grandmother.

She tried a new approach. "Look here Magpie, your elder is telling you to go away from here with your noisy argument."

Of course, Magpie was screaming so loud at Crow that he could not hear the grandmother either. When she could not get the attention of Crow or Magpie, she decided she would ask Eagle, most Wakhan Winged One, for his help. She had gotten her name, Bird Song, because she could sing out to the Winged Ones and they would answer her needs.

"Oh brother Eagle, I respectfully call on you. Please chase off these two noisy ones so our children can dream." Grandmother Bird Song called out.

With a mighty flap of his wings and a leap from the cliff, Eagle sailed towards the noisy pair. He gave a call of warning to Crow and Magpie as he came close. "Sskrreee".

They were so busy fighting they did not hear Eagle. It was as if their ears had closed up.

"Caaaw-caaaw, Caaaw-caaaw." Crow was screaming as he flapped his wings in the air so hard he was nearly falling off his perch.

"Kaaack-Kack-Kack." Magpie was yelling at the top of his lungs, as his wings too flapped up a storm.

When Eagle saw this, he yelled louder and came closer, "Sskrree, Sskrree" and that is when it happened.

Suddenly, both Crow and Magpie felt the contact of a sacred Eagle wing. At the same time, they saw a feather fall towards Mother Earth. They froze in mid squawk!

Oh no! What had they done? Crow swooped down and caught the feather before it landed on Mother Earth. As he came back to the branch, he heard Magpie speaking to Eagle.

Magpie was saying "Brother Eagle, most Wakhan of our family, I did not hear you so near or see your shadow. I am truly sorry for the injury I have caused you."

Crow was surprised to hear such an honorable thing come from the mouth of this rude Magpie neighbor.

"I have many times been a reckless bird, brother Eagle, but I think this might be the worst thing I have ever done. I am very sorry for my bad behavior." Crow spoke with dignity as he held Eagle's feather in one claw with is head bowed low.

Magpie was shocked! Could this be that unruly Crow who spoke with such respectful words? Magpie could hardly believe his ears. Crow handed the feather to Magpie, who was next to Eagle, so he could give it back.

As Magpie took the feather from Crows claw, their eyes met and with no words at all, they both knew that this mistake would not have happened if they had not been fighting. They knew they had not tried to listen at all; they had tried to out-scream each other rather that to work out a compromise.

Magpie spoke as he took the feather from Crow and said "I am ashamed, brother Eagle, that my loud talk and harsh words were more important to me than solving the problem that I thought I had with our cousin Crow" while he looked to Crow for a sign of understanding.

Crow took the feather back from Magpie and holding it respectfully he said, "We have disturbed the two-legged children and torn from your wing a sacred feather and now we return it to you with a request for your forgiveness and a promise to learn how to listen."

Eagle had watched all this with wise eyes and an open heart. He knew the lesson of listening had been learned by his little cousins and he saw that Bird Song, the Grandmother, looked on with learning in her eyes also.

He said to Crow "Give my feather to the Grandmother who watches from below, so that she might dress it with beads and leather and fur to make it even more beautiful. Let her keep it in her lodge and teach others to create this fine looking feather."

"We will call this sacred item a Talking Feather." Eagle said to Bird Song. "You have seen its power Grandmother. When these two held it, only truth and quiet wisdom came from their voices. Tell all the people that when they come together for Council or at any gathering where ears might be shut, to bring out the Talking Feather and let only the holder speak. This will be done in an honorable manner, letting everyone have his say. Begin with the highest ranking Elder and pass the feather until all have spoken, including the children, if they wish."

Eagle went on to explain, "When the feather is held with its back to the listeners and the inside curve to the speaker, he will hear his own words first as they come back to him. This will help to tame the harsh tongue of the two-legged. If disagreements are still between two people, they will turn the feather away from themselves so the words can go straight to the heart of the one they are at odds with."

"When all have spoken, a vote can be taken and the side who gathers the most votes will make the final decision" said Eagle.

As Eagle spoke these words, Crow brought the feather to the Grandmother. She was much honored to have learned this lesson. She took the feather to the lodge and every Grandmother listened as she told of the great thing she had just seen.

"That," said the oldest of the grandmothers, "is a very honorable vision, my wise friend. I can see how such a fine gift could help calm our young men and give voice to our wise Elders, who no longer carry the loud talk of youth."

"We shall honor this feather in a special way and dress it as Eagle has requested," said Bird Song.

"We will make a hole in a small limb to fit the quill and press it in with pitch to secure a handle." Bird Song smiled at the others.

"Then we can wrap the handle in leather from our graceful sister Doe or her protector Buck. We can put a bit of Coyote fur around the handle to remind us to always learn with humor and not to take ourselves too seriously" she chuckled.

"How about adding beads or other decorations that fit

the owner of this fine gift?" asked the Eldest Grandmother.

"I am sure that would make it even more Sacred," said Bird Song.

"There will be many times when people of all nations will struggle to be heard. Let us teach our children and our children's children, into the seventh generation (which we know means forever) how to make and use the Talking Feather" said another of the Grandmothers.

When Eagle's feather was fully dressed and the Grandmothers felt its power, they raised their voices in a song of gratitude to our most sacred Creator. The song brought sleepy-headed children to life all around them. There was much love and respect in that lodge on this special day.

Legend of the Dream Catcher

Tazz Connor was the great grand-nephew of the famous Chief Joseph of the Nez Perce tribe. He had been a family friend for years as a result of being in the US Navy during the Viet Nam era, where he served on the same base as my sister-in-law, Karen Limbaugh. When Karen introduced us he took a liking to me as his 'half-breed cousin' as he called me. After my divorce he was one of the few common friends our relationship who stayed connected.

Once when he invited me to a Sweat Lodge he was holding in his traditional Nez Perce way, I gifted him a Dream Catcher I had made. He told me that many tribes had adopted this sacred item from the Ojibwa people. He said he knew a legend from his childhood and wanted to share it with me. I do not know which tribe this legend came from, but he tossed in a few Lakota words to make it feel more familiar to me. Although he was fluent in his Nez Perce language he felt I would understand it better if he offered Lakota words because by this time he knew I was not going to learn his language no matter how often he tried to teach me.

I offer it here with his voice ringing in my ears and the light of his smile making shadows of memory in my heart.

Iktomi is an Indian name for spider. Iktomi is the web weaver and holds many great powers. It is believed that we walk a path on the web of life. The web connects us to all living beings. The words 'Mitakuye Oyasin' from the Lakota people means 'all my relations', and refers to all living beings. We are related because we all carry Creators breath in our spirits.

There is only one who creates life and He has given it to all his creatures great and small. The one who chooses which seed is viable and fertilizes the egg to bring new Winged Ones to Mother Earth, is the same one that gave you a heartbeat and me a breath. There is no life without this spark from the Creator of all things.

This means I am related to the Winged Ones, to those who Swim and those who Creep and Crawl and I am related to all Four Legged and Two Legged creatures. I am related to those who grow with roots in the ground like our Standing Tall Ones and our ancient stone grandmothers. I am related as well to the ones who live in the heavens known as the Star Nation. Iktomi is the one who keeps us connected through 'Mitakuye Oyasin' with the web of life.

In the days of our ancient ancestors there lived a great Pejuta Winan (medicine woman) who cared for the people of her village with wisdom and honor. She was called Waste Unci (good grandmother) by all her people. One day Ithanchan (chief) of her village came with a request. His young son Matho Ska (White Bear), who would one day be the chief, was suffering from lack of sleep.

If one does not sleep, one cannot receive the visions and dreams that teach us how to live our lives. It is believed to this day that we learn half our lessons during the dream time. Without his dreams, this youngster could never be a chief and lead his people for he would know only half himself.

What is the foolish pride of sleeping for only brief

hours when the body, mind, and spirit need the rest of dream time? Where is the value of walking through the day light with half closed eyes from lack of rest? Sleep is not a slothful thing, we are made in the image of our Creator, and even He rested on the seventh day!

When Ithanchan asked Waste Unci for help, she sent the chief to gather fresh bark from the aspen tree and told him to scrape the soft inner bark into a pot of boiling water and make a strong tea for his son to drink at bed time. The people have always known that the aspen tree bark, when made into a tea, is a great pain reliever and can help one to relax.

For three nights Matho Ska drank his tea just as Wi Ate (father sun) went to rest behind the hillside. When Wi Ate sleeps and brings darkness, it should be easy to slowly doze off and sleep. Matho Ska would begin to nod his head and sleep would start to creep in. But the boy could not stay asleep. He would awaken in a short time covered in sweat and shaking with fear. He did not want his family to worry about him, but knew he had to tell them he was still awake while the Star People danced in Mahpiya Ate (father sky) or they could not help him.

On the fourth morning, when he was still not sleeping, he told his father. When the chief heard this, he took his son to see Waste Unci.

She said, "Leave the boy with me for four days and he will return healed."

Matho Ska was a bit afraid of Waste Unci because she had so many odd looking things in her lodge and she always smelled of strange herbs and smoke. She was so very old and seemed to be smaller than even him, a boy of only ten summers. Her robe seemed to be too heavy for her and she had to bend over a bit to just carry it around. Her long white braids were nearly to her knees, or where he thought her knees should be if she were standing up straight. Her pale brown skin had so many wrinkles it looked like the top of his worn out moccasins.

She had no teeth, he noticed, when she spoke to him with a bit of a smile. She told him to lie on the Wapiti (elk) robe she had placed by her fire. He felt like a Hoksicala (baby), but he did as he was told. She began the Iktomi olowan (spider songs) with her old shaky voice, while softly drumming to a heartbeat rhythm. Soon he had fallen into a deep sleep and began to dream.

The dream was of a huge white bear, his name-sake, but it was very scary. The giant bear was chasing him and eating bits of his flesh as he ran and soon he yanked himself up from the dream and sat looking through sleepy, tear-filled, eyes at the fire, his small body shaking, but not from the cold night air. Waste Unci was nowhere to be seen. The dream had come to him for many nights and he was afraid to go back to sleep, for it would only be, to dream it all again. He sat looking at the flames and praying to Wakhan Tunkasila (sacred grandfather, God).

He said; "Please take this dream from my heart and give me rest, so that I might dream of good things for my people. Why does Matho Ska chase me? Am I not the one who is named for him? Does he think he should eat me up because I am not big enough to carry his name?"

Tears ran down the boy's cheek as he asked for the dream to leave him in peace. He was not as strong as his father and he was sure he could never lead his people with such wisdom.

Matho Ska had forgotten that he was still a child and had many winters to learn how to carry on the traditions of the people before he would be expected to do so.

For some, it is hard to know how we can walk the path Creator has offered us. Some choose to take a path that is harder than it needs to be because they are afraid to walk the path of wisdom. Some think to walk in war is easier than to walk in honor. Matho Ska had heard of the ones who spend a lifetime in anger or sadness, and he did not want to be counted among them.

Waste Unci suddenly appeared in his line of vision on the other side of the fire. Had she been there all this time and heard his prayer? Could she read his thoughts on the smoke that carried his prayer to Creator? She was looking softly at him and pretended not to see his tears. She told him she had just awakened from a dream of her own. This made him feel a bit more relaxed and he appreciated her for this show of respect.

She said, "Iktomi has told me how to create a web that will help you with your dreams. Tomorrow we will gather willow for this web." With that, she lay down and was soon snoring away while Matho Ska watched over the fire and fed it through the night.

Wi Ate was rising in the east, to wake up the day when Waste Unci gave out a last big groan and sat up to rub her old eyes, with the bony hands that Matho Ska thought looked more like sticks than fingers.

Without looking at him she said, "Go get a young limb from willow tree and make it into a small Changleska Wakhan (sacred hoop). Bring it to me with many lengths of sinew (thread like fiber from animal tendon)."

Matho Ska was so glad to be able to run from the lodge and into the fresh air that he had forgotten to say Tots-Ma-Wee (good morning) to Waste Unci in the words of his Nez Perce cousins. He first crept into his home lodge and quietly helped himself to sinew from his mother's sewing bag. He touched her cheek and she stirred from her sleep to nod her permission. She was sure Waste Unci must have requested the sinew. She saw the dark circles under her sons' eyes and knew he had not slept.

He quickly found a young willow branch and formed it into a small circle by bringing the ends together and tying them with some of the sinew. He soon stood before the lodge of his Pejuta Winan (medicine woman) and called out "Waste Unci, it is Matho Ska; I have made the Changleska

Wakhan (sacred hoop) of young willow and sinew. May I come in and show you?"

"Enter Hoksila (boy child) so we might create for you an Ihanbla (dream) catcher" she answered.

"In my vision from Iktomi she told me how to weave a web in this sacred hoop. It will work for you in the dream time" she said. As she spoke, her hands were carefully weaving the sinew inside the hoop made of willow and it began to look a bit like a spider web.

"Iktomi has explained to me how dreams that are not happy have very sharp points and sticky things hanging from them and dart around quick and angry," she said with a scowl on her face.

"The good dreams are smooth and soft, flowing with the rhythm of your breath. Iktomi says if you hang this dream catcher over your bed, the bad dreams will be stuck in the web and when Wi Ate shines, on them in the morning they will be gone like the morning dew from green grass. You will be glad to know that the sweet good dreams will flow through the web and feed your mind with all you need to learn." She spoke these things gently as her hands worked the sinew back and forth in the hoop.

Matho Ska was looking at his own hands in his lap as if they were unknown to him.

Waste Unci smiled and spoke softly "The good dreams will teach you how to be a mighty Matho Ska. Like the wise, White Bear of the North, who gave you his name, he will help you heal your people when they are sick, just like the killing cold of the North wipes out sickness and cleanses our Ina Makha (Mother Earth)" she spoke through her toothless mouth with a bit of a lisp.

"You will find food for the people, even in deep snow when it looks like none is there, just as Matho Ska of the North has always done. You will carry the linage of your father to many sons who will be great warriors and chiefs. The dreams you need to remember will flow to you from the web of life as you need them. Creator has a plan for all of his beings and as long as you honor Mitakuye Oyasin (all my relations), you will be blessed" she spoke gently to the boy.

Soon the web was finished and Waste Unci held it out to Matho Ska for examination while she said, "Take this with you as you walk today and when you find a feather you will know it is a gift to your dream catcher. Tie it on the left side and we will hang it so that becomes the West side for protection at night."

Matho Ska did as he was told and when the feather presented itself to him, he was glad to place it on his sacred hoop. He carried it to Waste Unci for her blessing, but she said "Rest this night in my lodge and we will see if the power has come to your Dream Catcher."

Matho Ska was awakened again that night, but he had noticed he woke before the great white bear had eaten any of his flesh. He had seen the bird that gifted him the feather flying beside him in his dream and helping him run faster. He had heard it call to him and warn him to run before the great giant bear could get too close.

The next day Waste Unci listened to the boy's new version of his dream. Then she told him, "We are not finished with your Dream Catcher. To give it more power, you must go into the world today and find a piece of fur. When you do, attach it to the top and we will call this North of your sacred hoop so it can help heal your wounds from the times when you were being eaten."

When Matho Ska had finished this days' work he had a nice piece of coyote fur. It was from one of the elder coyote cousins, who had chosen a place near Matho Ska's favorite thinking rock, as his final resting place. He felt that was a good sign and he again slept by Waste Unci's fire. This night, he was carried by the four-legged who had given him the fur, Coyote, and his bird friend had warned him of the great white bear before it got to him. He was happy to tell Waste Unci that he felt his dream was safe now and that it did not make him so afraid anymore.

She nodded her head and as if she had not heard a word he said. She told him "Today you will humble yourself. You will ask a gift of precious beads from a member of our tribe. Do not ask someone in your own family who would gladly make a gift to you. This should be a request from someone you may not feel comfortable asking. You will have to be humble and wise to make this request without offering payment. Anyone can trade for beads or work for a gift. This is to be a challenge to your heart. Find a person who may not know you well; someone you respect and honor with your thoughts and simply ask for the beads you need."

Matho Ska left the old woman's lodge with a heavy heart. Everyone knew he was the son of the Ithanchan, how could he ask for a gift and not dishonor his father? It might look as though his father could not supply his needs. He had spent three nights within the medicine lodge and Matho Ska felt his dreams were not so bad now. Could he keep the Dream Catcher and not add beads to it? Could he make beads from seeds or shells rather than feel like a beggar? Why did he need to be humbled? Had he been acting too big for his name?

He chose to think about this task while resting in the shade of an ancient Wakhan Wagachan (sacred cottonwood tree). He drifted off to sleep and began to dream. Soon he was running from the one he was named after. As he looked for his bird friend, he saw that it was flying too high to be of any help. He then began calling out to Coyote, his four-legged, fur covered cousin, but he was too far away to hear. As the flesh was torn from his shoulder, he came full awake with a breath sucked in too quick! His head was spinning and he felt like running away. He held his Dream Catcher close before his eyes and looked to see if any of his dreams had been caught. He knew it had not worked this time and felt angry with Waste Unci for getting his hopes up.

As he sat there feeling sorry for him-self, it came to

him that he must do this next thing and go ask for beads. He felt very small and afraid. He held his Dream Catcher in his hand and with trembling fingers took a deep breath then walked into the camp with determination.

"Creator, I will ask the first person I see and they will have what I need. Please give me the right words to speak," he prayed as he walked.

The very first person he saw was a young warrior he had hoped to hunt with someday. This man was a hero to many of the young boys in camp.

He had completed Hanblecheyapi (vision quest) when he was only 14 summers and had been on many hunts with the warriors of this village. This young man was so brave he probably never woke feeling afraid of his dreams no matter how scary they were. Matho Ska looked all around to see if someone else was there to speak to. He did not want to look foolish in this warrior's eyes. No one else was in sight, and he took this as a sign that Creator would give him the words to speak, as he had none of his own.

He stood before the young man and looked him directly in the eye. When he opened his mouth, he too wondered what he would say.

"Honorable warrior, may I speak from my heart to your heart?" He asked and heard his voice tremble.

"Of course little cousin" answered the young man with a bit of a grin.

"My name is Matho Ska; I am the oldest son of our chief and will someday take up the burden of this work for my father. I need to be very brave for this job and I am not," he said softly as his eyes lowered in shame.

"I would ask that you give me some beads from your hair that I can add them to this sacred hoop and gain strength from you who are brave enough for two men" Matho Ska held up the Dream Catcher as he spoke.

"I will honor your gift by using them to dress this sacred hoop to catch powerful dreams for our people" he spoke is a calmer voice.

"I know who you are" said the young warrior "and I know your father as a powerful leader. You honor me already with your words little cousin. I gladly gift you with these beads and will look forward to watching you grow brave as the summers pass until you are ready to walk your path." The young warrior said this as he began to remove some of the beads from his braids.

Matho Ska ducked his head in humble gratitude and mumbled "Thank you very much" as he turned and ran quickly up the hill to Waste Unci's lodge.

When Matho Ska returned to Waste Unci with his gift of beads, he told her of his nap under the tree of life and his dream. He spoke of his prayer and the words that were spoken to his hero. He held out the beads for her to add to his Dream Catcher. She placed them in the east to show that he would begin the birth of bravery just as Wi Ate is born fresh each morning from the east.

That night was the fourth and final night for Matho Ska to sleep in the old women's lodge. She blessed him and his Dream Catcher and hung it over his head from a lodge pole.

He was asleep before he could think about the events of this day. He dreamed of riding a fast horse and hunting Thathanka (Buffalo bull) with the young warrior he thought so highly of. He felt free and brave. His spirit bird flew close over his head as his four-legged helper, Coyote, ran by his powerful horse. When he woke, it was late in the morning and his father was there to walk him home.

"Oh Waste Unci I had the most wonderful, happy, beautiful dream. Should I tell you about it?" Matho Ska beamed as he spoke.

"No my young brave. This one is for you to keep in your heart. I am glad you were brave enough to do all that was required of you to make the Dream Catcher come to life for all our people. Now, when anyone needs protection in their dream time or needs help with capturing a healing dream, the Ojibwa people can help them," answered Waste Unci.

"We know that only half of life is lived on the awaking side, which is where the lessons are taught. The half lived in dream time is the half where learning takes place. Grow in spirit always Matho Ska, for you are becoming a great White Bear" instructed Waste Unci.

This legend has been shared with many tribes throughout the country and each group may have its own version of the story, but the main purpose of the Dream Catcher is always the same. No matter who the dreamer or the teacher may be, it is always Iktomi who has shown someone how to weave a web to catch the bad dreams and promote the good ones.

Chipmunk, Snake and Fire

Nez Perce

This great story as told by Tazz Conner gets lots of laughter and oohs and ahhs when the storyteller uses sound effects and different voices for each character. Not just from the children either! Tazz was pretty good at this, but always cracked himself up when he made hissing snake sounds. His chuckles and Indian accented English made this one of our favorites.

During the long cold winter, in the days before man, Chipmunk and Snake had an arrangement. They would stay together by their friend Fire for the cold months of snow. They would build a Tipi over Fire to protect him from Wind.
Snake would be quiet and docile all winter long because Chipmunk never helped him turn over by Fire. His one cold side kept him quiet and not hungry at all. The log for Fire to feed on all winter was so thick it would take all those long cold months to burn through. Fire was in no hurry for the warm weather of Spring. He liked burning day and night at a soft and flickering pace. Now Chipmunk had a grand stash of nuts in this Tipi so she was never hungry either.
They all did well with this arrangement over the cold of winter. But before the tree log burned through to signal spring Chipmunk got tired of the old dry nuts from winter's

storage. She loved to chatter to someone, just anyone, but these two were boring. She dreamed of running up tree trunks and chasing her cousins round and round. She began to wonder if the log was too thick and maybe spring was here. She chose to sneak out one day while Fire was low and Snake was sleeping.

Chipmunk slipped under the Tipi door and scampered down the log that was feeding Fire. She ran over frozen clumps of snow and jumped over thawing mud puddles. Down the mountain side she ran looking for signs of spring.

When she got to the meadow it was filled with nice green grass! Spring had come to the valley. She ate the grass until her tummy was full. She sat on a nice warm rock and tried to think what to say, before she ran back to the Tipi. If she told these two that spring was here it could be dangerous. Snake might get back his energy and eat her up. Fire might think he was tired after all winter and go out while it was still cold and windy in this early spring. She had to think of a story before she could return. She made herself walk slowly back to her warm home.

She had just come in through a little hole in the back of the Tipi when Snake woke up. "Hisss it daylight" he hissed?

"I'm not sure, but it could be, we slept very sound last night. I did not hear a thing did you? I thought I did but it was just a twig scratching the tipi from the wind. It must be awful cold out there and I bet the sun has nearly forgotten how to shine and, and..." chattered Chipmunk.

"Huuussshhh" said Fire "I am nearly out of wood, should I spread my light, or is spring here?"

Snake liked to hear Fire talk. His hhuussshhh sound was almost like snake's own hhiiiss and it felt good. He could hardly tolerate that chatter box Chipmunk and he was just waiting for his strength to return so he could eat her up in one big bite!

"Ssssmellss like grassss on someonesss breath" hissed

snake.

"Pop, Snap, Huuuummm I thought I smelled it too" said Fire.

"Oh no, that couldn't be or that would mean someone went outside and found it was spring and then didn't share the news. Oh who would do that? It could not have been you Fire because if you went out you would go out! Oh tee hee, hee I have made a joke and it could not be you Snake because you have no strength and it was not me" she chattered with her fingers crossed behind her back.

"I am getting ssstronger every day and I am sssso hungry sssso I better not find ssssomeone telling ssstoriesss to my empty belly," said Snake.

"Aye, I feel the shhame way" drawled out Fire. For he was running low on wood and trying to hang on till spring.

Chipmunk tried to turn her head away when she spoke so her breath could not be noticed and she said "I have a plan I will go because I am young and fast and wide awake and I can see if it is spring yet and then scurry right back here to tell you if it is safe for you to sleep Fire and for you to come out in the sun Snake" she chattered on quickly while looking up and around at the Tipi walls so as not to breathe on Snake.

"Now you don't need to worry because if it is still winter I will know as soon as I pop my head out of the Tipi and if it is looking like spring I will run quickly to the meadow and then back here as fast as I can. You do not need to make a move or try to follow me at all. I am a very fast runner. Of course it is a long way to the meadow so don't worry if I am gone a while."

And with that she scampered out the front door. The only reason she had come back to the Tipi was for warmth on chilly nights and to collect her stash of nuts. But it would have been a giveaway for her story if she began packing her cheeks full of nuts, so she just gave them back to Mother

Earth and ran as fast as her legs could go.

When she ran out so fast Snake hissed to Fire "Ssshhe did smell like grassss and ssshe lied to ussss." With a flip of his tail he knocked over Chipmunks stash of nuts and they fell into Fire. Fire was so excited about the new fuel he leapt with joy.

A snap and crackle gave a rich new voice to Fire and he boasted, "Shhhhe won't be safe out there in the cold. With all these dry nuts I will have plenty of food. I am so large Pop, Snap, now I can reach a new place on this log." He said as he stretched out his flame arms and wrapped around another big piece of wood.

The extra warmth from Fire gave Snake a fresh jolt of energy. He was warmed on all sides and could wiggle quickly as you please around that Tipi. He wiggled over to where Chipmunk and been sitting "Sssure enough SSShe wasss lying! Here isss a piece of grassss to prove it!" hissed Sake as he flipped the rest of her nut stash onto Fire.

Fire leaped up so high his flames caught the Tipi on fire. Now Snake was in a hurry. He wiggled as quick as he could to get out of the Tipi before it burned down and Fire was so filled with glory at his own flame that he began to leap from the Tipi to the grass and sure enough it was spring!

Snake turned back to Fire "Thanksss for the warm winter, I'm off to find that Chipmunk for my breakfast." He called as he wiggled away.

Fire called back on his roaring voice "Thank you for feeding me all winter, aww pop, snap, so I might live again this fine spring day!"

Chipmunk had run as far as she could. After being awake all night and feeding full on grass she was out of energy. Besides she felt bad about misleading her winter companions. She stopped to look back and then she saw it!

The Tipi was burning up and Fire was dancing in his hot suit to the meadow where she was and right in front of him was that nasty old Snake. She suddenly realized they knew she had lied and with the spring wind blowing towards her she was in trouble.

"Cheeeeep" she screamed and ran a crazy zig-zag path all the way to the grassy meadow and over a downed limb across the creek. She hoped Snake did not know this way. Finally she made it to the nut tree which had no nuts only new leaves and she leaped up its branches chattering as she ran from branch to branch to the very top. From there she could see that Fire was calmer now having reached the damp grass and as he ate the fresh grass he grew lazy and had forgotten to chase her anymore.

That old Snake had been on the run while Fire kept him warm but now he had to stop and lay in the sun for energy. But he was happy as he munched on fresh grass too. Finally she knew she was safe. But for the rest of her days she had dreams and visions of being burned up be Fire and eaten by Snake because of her crooked chatter tongue. Sometimes if you listen when you walk in the woods, you can still hear her chatting about the long winter with Snake and Fire.

Nez Perce Sweat Lodge

Another fine legend shared by Tazz with his own brand of humor mixed in goes something like this...

The One Made of Sticks walked the land from end to end. He knew all the animals. The ones that swam in the ocean and those that swam in the rivers, lakes, and ponds. He knew all the ones with four legs and those that crept or crawled. He knew everyone that lived on the land.

One day when the One Made of Sticks was walking, Creator told him some news. Creator called all the animals he had made and they came together. The One Made of Sticks rubbed his hands together very fast and started a nice fire. He tossed in twigs that fell from his hair as they sat around his fire. In those days all the animals were friends. No one ate the other and they were not afraid. Wolf was friend of Rabbit and Deer let Coyote babysit her fawns. Mouse flew on Eagle's wing and Frog played with Fly. There was no fear and there was no death.

That day when the Walking Around Stickman called, they all sat close as cousins do. "The Great Mystery who created us all has told me about a new time. There is a creature coming that only has two legs, he is called Man. These two-legged people are not strong like us so we will need to teach them. Creator says we all should help. Some of us will taste death so we can feed the People," said

Walking Around Stick man.

"What is death they asked?"

That is when we 'Cross the Great River' to go home to our Creator.

"That sounds good to me," said one.

"And me too" said the others.

"We must choose names so the people will know who we are," said the Man Made of Sticks.

"Come forward, Tall One with Big Antlers, and let us see who you will be," said the One Made of Sticks.

"I want to be Elk. The people can call me Wapiti and they can eat me too. I will let them make clothes of my fine pelt and moccasins from my hides. They can make tools from my horns and I will teach them many lessons. I want to be Elk because that is who I am."

"Well" said the Stick One to the rest "How will we know if this is right?"

"Let him show us how he is Elk," They said.

So Elk took mighty leaps and ran gracefully about the field. He laid his fine antlers over his back and ran through the forest without a scratch. He ran back to the fire and stopped to stand still as a tree.

"He looks like Elk to me," said the One Made of Sticks.

"He is Elk," said the others.

Then the Big Bird of Powerful Feathers came forward and he said, "I am Eagle and I want to stay as Eagle. But the two-legged People will feed on me in spirit only and not eat my body. They will learn much from my lessons and they will honor each of my feathers."

"Well let's see if you are Eagle," the animals said.

He flew into the sky circling so high they could not see him. Then the One Made of Sticks called out "Where are you?"

Like a shot arrow, he flew straight down and then his mighty tail tucked under and his wings waved backwards. He stopped with a hop in front of the fire with his head held high.

"Am I Eagle?" he asked.

"Yes" they all called out loud.

That is how we know he is Eagle and he took the sacred name Wambli that very day.

Then came one of the small dog tribe and he said, "I am Coyote and I will be a friend to the People who are coming."

Everyone laughed because they knew Coyote was a trickster and he made up stories all day long. They knew he would make the People laugh but he would not be their friend. He would steal their food and run off with their hides but he would be full of stories and that would be good.

"Aaaaye this one is Coyote for already he tells a story" laughed the Old Wise Bird.

All the others said, "Aye he is Coyote!" and they all laughed some more.

Then someone said, "That was a wise thing to say so you must be Owl."

"Hoot me?" asked Owl and they all laughed again.

When all the animals had come, one by one, to the fire and taken a name, the Stick Man said, "Now you will not be as one tribe. You will each stay with your own cousins and will sometimes fight each other and even eat each other."

That was when they all ran off to live in different places and became cautious of each other. And rightly so, for now Wolf would eat Rabbit and Coyote would chase Deer so all the days of perfect peace were no more.

Then the One Made of Sticks went to the river bank and to the ocean shore and he did the same game of naming with those who swim. They began to feed on one another and some went to live in the hot waters of the south and others to the cold waters in the north. They were not of the same tribe any more.

Then that One Who was Made of Sticks went to the

Creepy Crawlies and said, "You too must take up names and find your place among those People that are coming."

The Ant tribe knew how they could teach about hard work and community and Bee also knew he could teach about co-operation. They all took names that day and went to live in all the tiny places.

When the last of the Bird tribe finished with the naming ceremony the One Made of Sticks said, "I am tired but I have been blessed with all the animal spirits. How will I serve the two-legged People that will come?"

As he lay resting on the ground he noticed that a circle between his many legs was filled with lessons. There was strength from his years of growth and wisdom from Owls friendship. There was laughter from Coyote and tenderness from Deer. He saw grace from Elk and family from Ant. He could see winter rest from Bear and hear songs from all the little Creepy Crawlies night voices.

As he stood there thinking of all these good medicines he felt a warmth under his belly. One of his friends from the Stone Tribe had rolled out of the hot belly of Mother Earth and came to rest with his friends in the middle of the Stick One. As the Stick Man saw the glow from the heated stone and felt the sweat from his limbs he knew what he would do and for the first time he knew his name.

He is called Inipi by those of the Sioux and in all languages he is known as Sweat Lodge. The many lessons from Mytakwe Oyasin (all my relations) are held in sacred space in this lodge. The Stick Man has been covered over with blankets to hold in the warmth of the Stone Tribe and it has rounded his rough shape. Now he is as the womb. Inipi holds a small door open to invite the People in. They must be humble and crawl on hands and knees to enter.

When the Stone Tribe has warmed the inside of the lodge, it makes the People sweat. They are cleansed and made well by this sweat. When they have offered prayers and sang songs they crawl out of the womb in re-birth and are again pure before Creator.

A Creation Story

Every tribe has their own creation story and many have a variety of renditions of the same legend. The first time I heard this legend was from my father Chas Thompson. He loved to talk and enjoyed the sound of his own voice. He even tape recorded himself many times while giving lectures, political speeches and when telling stories and legends. He did not credit this legend to any particular tribe at the time, other than to say it was not the Santee or Dakota creation story.

Years later I read one very similar to this in one of Jami Sam's books, which leads me to believe this story is based loosely on the Cherokee traditions. There is also a good dose of the Christian creation story woven between the traditions, so it is possible this was a version created after native children were placed in Catholic schools. My father was placed in the "Father Flannigan's Home for Boys" when he was twelve years old and might have heard the legend from that source. He also went to seminary school in the Adventist faith for a few semesters. In his later years he was active in a local Christian community church.

There is also a hint of Shamanic Journey work involved as they enter the below lands through the hollow tree. In any case it has some wonderful lessons for children and adults about how we should treat one another. It is written here in my words but comes from the memory of hearing it told in the voice of my father. Whether he learned it from an unknown source or made it up himself, I find it beautiful.

Creator of all things is a Great Mystery, even to everything that It created. It has always been and will always be, with no beginning and no ending. The Creator of everything is not male or female, but is both, and yet neither. It is the largest of all large things and the smallest of all small things. The Creator of all that is has no boundaries and is forever. Creator is sometimes called the Great Spirit or Great Mystery, because two-leggeds cannot begin to know all of Creator's ways.

We Indian people believe that everything on the earth and in the earth and even the earth itself is made by the Creator. Some of our people call this Creator "Wakhan Tunkasila", which means Sacred Grandfather. This is because the Creator teaches us everything we need to know, just as the beloved grandfather teaches the next generation, but does not teach us the mysteries of how to 'create' life.

We say Sacred Grandfather because He is the one of forever and not the Grandfather of this life. We do not say father because the father is the one of sometimes unfair discipline. He makes rules and laws to please his needs and will punish the child who breaks them. The Sacred Grandfather makes guidelines that serve our best interest and helps make us more worthy. Wakhan Tunkasila is always fair and could never hate his children or punish us unfairly.

Wakhan Tunkasila teaches our heart to beat and our lungs to breath. It teaches us to move our arms and legs even before we are born. It makes our belly accept the milk and tells our body how to grow. It teaches us to feel pain and to feel love. It teaches us to cry and to laugh. All of these things we learn before language. This Creator is bigger than any religion or even modern science. It is so big that we two-leggeds cannot understand It. So this is our legend, made of our ideas about how two-leggeds came to Mother Earth. Only you can know if it is true.

Creator looked one day at the Star People that He had made. They were very beautiful and they smiled back at Him with great light in their eyes. He called loudly from his heart voice.

"Oh my children of the Sky, I am coming this day to capture a bit of your glory."

And the Star People said, "We are yours, as you have made us, our Star Nation belongs to you Creator. As we shine in darkness with sister Moon and hide in day light from brother Sun, we never forget that we were made for your pleasure. What can we do to serve you?"

"I wish to gather the dust of your brightness and from it I will create another being in our heavens," Creator sang.

The Star People shown even more brightly for this opportunity to serve the Great Mystery who is the Creator of everything. So with joy in His heart and gladness in His voice Creator reached to the heavens and took a bit of glory from each of the Star People, which made them even more beautiful. By offering a portion of themselves they had a bit of space left open and as they turned in the dark night sky it caused a magic thing, from a distance they twinkled in their brightness. That is how it works sometimes, when you give of yourself, you become more beautiful. The Star People are still blinking and twinkling in the sky to remind us of this lesson.

Creator drew the bits of Star dust to His breast and squeezed it tightly in His hands. Soon it became a ball of molten light that seemed as liquid gold. Creator set it free in the heavens with a little spin and blew His sacred breath upon its face and 'First World' was born.

Now the molten Star bits became firm on the surface as they cooled from Creators breath. A crust covered and protected the molten center where lives the heartbeat of Creator.

The Great Mystery said, "I will call you Ina Makha which means Mother Earth because you will be a mother to many creations that I dream."

This is how we know the name of our land; she is called Mother Earth for she bore many children of every kind imagined by our Creator. As He gave her this sacred name He wept with joy. His mighty salty tears gathered in pools at each end of Ina Makha and Creator called them Oceans.

Sea shores were born and the Stone People could be seen lining the beaches. These Stone People were the first of Creators beings to live on the land and inside Mother Earth. He told them they were the bones of Mother Earth and would hold her together with power and wisdom. They had no legs for traveling and no voices for speaking but in their silent stationary lives they could record all the magic of The Great Mysteries creations.

Creator called the Stone Nation, Inyan Oyate and said they were His legend keepers, for they would record the history of everything that happened on all the lands.

From the smooth and crusted surface of Ina Makha, Creator formed creatures of all kinds. He made Winged Ones to fly above the land and brush the sky with graceful feathers of every color. He made every kind of four-legged creature to walk in beauty upon the land. Some were made to eat each other but most were made to eat from the hair of Ina Makha's land. This lush green hair grew everywhere, to feed all the four leggeds and this green hair's seed would feed the flying ones.

Creator made Creepy Crawlies for walking close to the land. By showing the Creepy Crawlies how to live fast and short lives and then feedback their bodies to Ina Makha, much dirt was made to nourish even more of the Rooted Tribe.

Sacred herbs were made by Creator to provide food and medicine for all the living ones on Ina Makha.

Creator told the Ant Tribe, one of the Creepy

Crawlies who was most industrious, "You will one day have a most honored job to do, so do not feel less than others because of your size. I have made you just the right size for your real job. For now go below the surface of Ina Makha's glorious hair and build your selves great villages filled with children." And they did.

Creator made the Standing Tall Ones. They were shown how to dance in the wind with their mighty arms wide open and how to hold the Winged Ones homes safe in their branches. He taught them to reach deep into Mother Earth and wrap their roots around the huge boulders of Stone Nation. He taught some of the Standing Tall ones to offer their leaves back to feed Mother Earth each fall and others he taught to hold tight their needles through the winter snows. Creator had filled the land of Ina Makha with all good things.

Creator smiled on the great Oceans and all form of swimming things came to life. With a powerful touch of His finger many mountains were born and valleys were filled with lakes and rivers that ran to the great oceans and swimming ones of the fresh water were made real in a blink of His eye.

It was beautiful and Creator said to the Star People, for they could hear his voice, "I will make a two-legged, one who can stand on Ina Makha and see this beauty and be grateful for this work I have done. They will often look on your beauty and marvel at the glory of your magic."

And the Star People were so happy they leaped and shot across the great sky in their joy.

Then Creator took dust from Ina Makha and mixed it with His love. The Great Mystery breathed His sacred breath on First Mans' face and said, "You will walk the Red Road with Me." which meant he would travel close to Creator's heart.

First Man asked "How else could I walk Great Mystery, most Wakhan (Sacred) of all and Creator of everything?"

This gave Creator such happiness that He shed tears of joy and the first rains fell upon Ina Makha. His mighty tears gathered in sacred pools and stayed warm and steamy to offer healing to all His creatures, including 'First Man'. The medicine held in these sacred hot springs is direct from Creators tears of joy. Many of the Winged and four-legged know to come lay in the sacred waters for healing. First Man taught all who would listen to come to the sacred hot pools for wellness. First Man knew that many from the Stone Tribe had healing wisdoms as well. Many of the medicines from these sacred waters were trapped in the Stone Tribe and were ready to serve wherever they were needed.

All was well for many moons and then First Man became lonely.

Creator felt his longing and came to First Man saying, "You need a mate just as all my creatures have. You need a gentle one to teach you balance and harmony. You are strong and powerful in many ways, but you need to find your softness." So Creator made First Woman.

When First Man and First Woman came together there was such happiness that all the Winged Ones of the skies began to sing.

Creator said to First Man and First Woman "You are so wonderful, you have given my Winged Ones song. You may go and have children and grandchildren and fill Ina Makha with many songs."

They soon gave Owl, Wolf and Coyote songs for the night. They gave all the little Winged Ones sweet happy voices for the dawn. The great Winged Ones like Wambli (Eagle) took a mighty shrill voice to call from on high and warn of his arrival.

The laughter First Man and First Woman shared was copied by Creepy Crawlies who chirped day and night in gladness. The mighty Wind chose a strong and roaring voice to match the powerful song of Ocean. The land was filled with much song and laughter and with many children and the children's children until seven generations played in harmony and love on Ina Makha.

It was during this time that the two-leggeds began to forget. They were blessed with all the food and many waters of pureness from Creator's happy tears, so they did not need to ask for help. They had no reasons to be forgetful; they just became lazy and forgot. They had forgotten where they came from and they had become neglectful of Ina Makha and the ones who lived there with them. They did not tell stories or legends in those days so it was easy to forget.

First Man stopped going to the sacred places of hot water for healing. He became sore in his body but only would complain and would not help himself to wellness. First Woman became lazy and sat all day being fed by her daughters and becoming demanding as if she were their Creator saying things like "I gave birth to you so you must take care of me."

The People took herbs from the breast of Ina Makha and left no gifts or prayers of gratitude. They argued over who could sit nearest the fire and who could dance in the mountains and who would sleep in the desert. They became selfish and never spoke of gratitude to the One who had made them all.

This made Creator sad and when finally his patience had worn through he shook his head and his long white braids made Ina Makha shiver. In her shivering she began to break apart and to push up hills and mountains and gouge out deep canyons and valleys where smooth plains had once been. Some were toppled over and then scraped flat on top by the wind from Creators braids.

These new mountains groaned and complained and spewed out hot melted stones from the heart place of Ina Makha. Great cracks in the surface of Ina Makha became canyons with roaring angry waters tearing at the earth.

As Ina Makha began to quake and crumble the Winged Ones went to Sky for protection and the Creepy

Crawlies began to crawl to their hiding places. The Stone Tribe, on whose back the dirt and grasses and Standing Tall Ones lived began to roll into piles, making caves and hidden places to provide safe havens for many of the four-legged ones.

The land of Ina Makha broke apart and drifted on the mighty oceans as islands. Some went North and some South and they even separated East from West. These land masses were a part of the whole body of Ina Makha but now they lived apart from the whole. These great lands were separated by many Ocean waters and the ones living on them were changed.

While all this was happening the Two Legged ones ran from place to place but could not find safety. This is when they learned about death. Many of them gave their breath of life back to Creator that day.

But Creator loves the Two Legged and called out to Ant. "Ant this is your Sacred Day. Go find First Man and First Woman, I will make them small like you, and you can protect them in your mighty village below. You can teach them your wisdom ways for this is the day you were made for."

When Ant found First Man and First Woman they were already becoming small so he led them to the sacred hollow tree. This ancient one was standing over the door way to Ants village in the below world.

Ant said to First Man, "Come with me and bring your mate as Creator has planned. You will be safe and you will learn much from those who live below." First Man and First Woman gladly followed Ant below the surface and down deep into Mother Earth.

As Ant led them down the traveling trail into the great village of the world below, First Man and First Woman became frightened by the dark.

Soon they met a lowly worm with no arms or legs and no eyes, who told them. "If I can crawl on my belly in humbleness for all my life, with no eyes and feel only security from my Creator's heart, I would think such beings as you could easily feel safe in his care. There is no darkness where Creator lives, so follow Ant and do not be fearful."

First Man was ashamed and did not complain more. He became a stoic man that day and learned to be more tolerant of discomfort and to realize the circumstances of his life were of his own making. Soon their eyes were given the night vision and they could see where they were walking. They traveled down the mighty roots of the Standing Tall hollow tree. They looked up and saw the roots of the Rooted Ones (plant tribe) protecting them. They saw Iktomi (spider) keeping her eggs and children safe from harm in this darkness. It was a long walk, but they finally stood before the Stone Tribe.

The Chief of Stone Tribe rolled in front of First Man and First Woman. He bumped his body into his mate and the clicking sound of their bodies made his voice. They could understand this tapping as his words.

He told them "Do you see how we must work together to make our voice? You must learn about working together and always be in good relations with your Creator. Because you forgot who made you and you forgot how to be grateful, this terrible time has come to Ina Makha. It is hard for her to give birth in this way. I will write the story of this day on my own body of how this has pained Our Mother, so you will never forget."

First Man and First Woman saw all the 'below' people living in harmony with Creator's plan and they were sorry for not teaching their own children better. Now they would not see their children again and they hung their heads in shameful tears. By spoiling their children and forgetting to be grateful they had caused the destruction of the very ones they loved.

Stone People began to educate First Man and First Woman in many things. They were shown how to shape the stone called obsidian to create arrow tips for easier hunting. They learned to use the Stone People to grind corn and sacred herbs for medicine. They were shown how to make a sacred altar from the stone people's bodies. They were taught how to do ceremony upon this alter as a way of remembering to be grateful. The sacred altar was dressed with many fine things from the new world where they lived. They knew this altar would be seen each day and could help them to remember about being grateful to Creator.

First Man and First Woman had a good life with the Ant Tribe and were learning much from the Stone Nation about their heritage. These wisdom keepers were showing them all of the history from the day Creator gathered Star dust until the day Creator was saddened by them. During these years they had many children and their children had children until the seven generations were living together under the blanket of Mother Earth.

First Man told First Woman "We should make stories that will become legends to tell our children just as the Stone Nation has told us. This is a good remembering tool."

"Yes" said First Woman "and we will teach them to build altars and to honor all things. We must let them know that we have cousins that are Creepy Crawlies and Stone People so they will know to respect everything Creator has made. We must tell them that we are all relatives."

First Man said, "You have grown wise my mate and I am glad we can be better teachers now. I think we need a special word for all of Creators beings" and he said "Mitakuye Oyasin" which means 'all my relations'. "This word will be used by the people so we will remember we are related to Ina Makha and all her children."

One day Creator called to Grandfather Ant for Ant had aged in these many years and asked in a silent voice only Ant could hear, "Do you think my Two Legged People have learned from this lesson?"

"Yes" answered Grandfather Ant. "They have learned

many ceremonies and have seen much history recorded by the Stone People. They have learned from all of your teachers. They have stories and legends and sacred words. They have made altars for remembering gratitude and are much wiser than before they came here. I believe they are ready to come to the next world if it pleases you."

Creator called in a song from Ina Makha's heartbeat to First Man and First Woman asking them to come to the surface. At first they were so very excited, for they could remember the glory of Ina Makha and all her beings. Then they became afraid for their children and their children's, children.

"Will they be able to see in the light of your glory, oh Great Creator?" They asked.

"If there was not a safe place for them, I would not call you. Leave your fear behind, like worm taught you and come let me see you," said Creator.

First Man and First Woman went to all the generations and told them of this great blessing. Some were not sure what this would mean and others ran to pack their things. But First Man said in his wisdom, "No my family, leave all that you have been blessed with here, for when we walk to the surface we will become tall and strong again and all these small things that served us well here will be too small for you to even see. Have a generous heart and gift them to our Ant cousins. You will have more abundance on the surface of our new world than you can imagine. There will be foods and clear water like you have never seen. There are many living things to show you great beauty and bright light all day long from your brother Sun. Sweet sister Moon will shed soft light for the night with her Star cousins. There will be no total darkness in the above land. You will meet 'all your relations' Mitakuye Oyasin."

This seemed to the People to be another one of the Grandfather's stories, and not real for he had told of the life above, many times. But the children thought it just a legend.

They had learned respect and honor from First Man and First Woman so they obeyed the elders and gave away their possessions and walked the trail to Ina Makha's surface.

Sure enough as they climbed up the path on twisted Hollow Tree's roots they saw the fine hair roots overhead from the sacred herbs growing above just as First Man had told them. They met Iktomi and all her family living in her web near the roots.

They heard her whisper. "You have a web of remembering in your hearts. Bring the lessons from below to this new middle world so we can all live in harmony."

Soon they could feel their bodies growing in size. The children and the children's children were amazed and became very curious. The excitement began to grow as the People came near the surface. They realized that First Man and First Woman had told those stories and legends about a real place. This is how we know most legends come from real places.

After a while, Grandfather Ant told First Man "You know the way from here, just up those roots and out Hollow Tree to the surface. I am old and my legs are tired. I leave you to lead your people now, do so in humbleness and respect and they will honor you all your days."

First Man and First Woman had become friends to Grandfather Ant and would miss him. He told First Man "When you come to the surface you will have grown to your full size and will not visit me here again. You can help my people and I will help yours even though we can never speak again."

"How can this be?" asked First Man.

"When you reach the middle world, turn and look back and you will notice the Stone People everywhere. Choose one to stay with you always as a reminder of our days together. Make a soft deer skin pouch and hang it around your neck so it will lie on your heart. This will help you remember to always be grateful for the blessings of

Creator," said Grandfather Ant.

"Yes I can do that and it will help me remember all the lessons you and Inyan Oyate (Stone Nation) have taught my people," said First Man.

First Woman was proud of her mate for his wisdom. "How can I ever repay you for the hospitality you have shown my children until this seventh generation?" First Woman asked Grandfather Ant.

"Remember your legends and make songs for your stories. When Buffalo, Deer, or Elk lay down their sacred breath to feed your people, think of us. When the dogs have finished with the bones you could lay them on our hill at the base of Hollow Tree and we will find much food on these bones, as we are so small. We will return to you clean white bones so you can make many tools. And you will help feed all the Creepy Crawly Tribe." said Grandfather Ant.

"This will be another lesson about gifting for our people. Thank you, old friend. I will hold you in my heart for all the moons of my life," said First Man, as he turned to lead his people to the surface.

As they climbed the root pathways of the mighty Hollow Tree of life they began to grow even larger. Soon they could take longer steps and they were very near middle world.

First Man told the people "You will see light for the first time when we reach the surface. It may burn your eyes, so be careful not to look up at our Sun brother. He will soon bake all our skin to the wonderful earthen red color that was given to us by Creator, when life was new. No longer will we be frail and transparent. We will be servants to our Creator with much strength and happiness. Soon your eyes will be strong as those of Wambli (Eagle) and you will see for great distances."

First Man was a little fearful for his people as they stepped to the surface, but he remembered the bravery of Worm and walked tall.

The generations were not sure if this was all real or legend, but they chose to believe in First Man's story. First Man walked with no fear as he reached the surface and he knew this was the Second World.

When he turned back he saw one of Stone Tribes most beautiful gems. It shown with light in its heart and he gave it the name Crystal for he knew it had many healing ways to teach the people. He made a pouch of deer skin and placed the sacred stone over his heart. This is how so many people know to wear sacred items over their hearts. Some make medicine pouches; some make necklaces. Some even make rings and place them on the heart finger. All the people know to use the Stone Tribe to honor one another and Creator.

The light was not as bright as First Man remembered and then he realized Creator, the most Wakhan Tunkasila (sacred grandfather) of all, had blessed them by leading them to the surface at night time. With the soft glow of Sister Moon, they could easily begin to see in the light again.

"Oh Great Mystery, Creator of everything, we come humbly and gratefully to your feet. We bow before your glory and thank you for the many lessons and all the protection you have given us these many long generations," said First Man.

"We are grateful that you would spare our eyes the brightness of day by delivering us here on Owl's song to bow before you with Sister Moon. Her fullness will lead us to dawn in gentleness." Said First Woman, knowing she could trust her Creator to protect her family.

Creator was greatly pleased with this show of honor and respect and their expressions of gratitude. However, he could hear fear in their voices and wished to have it replaced with faith and love, so he spoke gently to First Man and First Woman saying, "I have missed you my Two Legged treasures. You have helped me name the many animals I created and you gave joy and song to them. Their songs have kept my heart from breaking while you were gone. I see you have learned of respect, honor, and ceremony as a way of expressing your gratitude. I gift you all of Ina Makha for your home."

When Creator had spoken he poured out pure love on all his people and they felt comfort in this love.

Creator said to them "You had a hard time learning the lessons of gratitude. I hope you have learned to give gifts and be hospitable to one another and Mitakuye Oyasin. Think of your friends from the Ant tribe and how they welcomed you and provided for all your needs. Remember how Iktomi told you to weave 'remembering' into your hearts. Remember how Worm taught you to have no fear. Remember how Ant taught you many things about living in harmony as one tribe. Always know that Stone Nation has the legends of your generations written on his face. Remember how they cared for you with great hospitality and generosity. Live in this way always and much joy will fill your lodges."

Just as the soft dawn was breaking First Man and First Woman gave their promises to Creator that they would honor his wishes of remembering and turned to East for morning ceremonies. They would honor East as the direction from where all newness and all birth of each day lives. When they spoke of East they would know that the yellow color of Brother Sun peeking over the horizon would represent the change from darkness to light. The lessons of East would remind them of new beginnings. They were grateful for this new life on the Second Earth.

There was much feasting and celebration among the people. The children and grandchildren of First Man and First Woman had never seen colors so bright or felt Wind on their faces. They had never eaten the gifted meat of Buffalo nor tanned his hide. They learned from their grandparents how to know who was singing the songs and what the names of all the animal tribes were. They learned to make drums and dance with Ina Makha's heartbeat.

These were exciting days when new knowledge came quickly to the descendants of First Man and First Woman. Many children were born and their parents told them about the years when they lived in the below world but the new children's children thought it was just a legend and were not sure if Creator could do such a thing.

The People were good to remember their ceremonies and they became traditions that were passed down for all the generations until this day. The People grew rich in furs and Tipis and had much dried food stored for the winters. They could always find Buffalo and Deer who would lay down their bodies and give their spirit breath back to Creator so they could feed the People.

There was time for playing games and even time for making beautiful things to wear. There would have been time for storytelling and legends if anyone had wished to hear. Soon the People had spread out over Ina Makha and many were making new languages. They all had their own wealth to bargain with. When the seasons were right, the People would gather and have feasting and dancing and trade their goods. Over the years, the People began to forget the remembering and some began to be selfish.

First Man remembered Crystal and took her from his pouch. He tipped her side to side in Sun's bright light and looked into her shining places. He watched her hidden rainbows dance across his hand.

He asked her "How can I make these children well again? Is it too late to tell the legends?"

Crystal answered from her heart. "First Man, you have received many lessons. You have been gifted much but you are not strong in your heart for you have not enough love. How could you tell all the generations what you should have told your sons? When you truly love others, you offer discipline as well as blessings. You must remember to teach the hard lessons with the soft ones."

First Man began to worry about the generations and watched closely to see if Creator was pleased or not. He began to recognize fear in his heart and worry in his mind.

The people from all generations were doing the ceremonies and being grateful for Creators abundance, but they were starting to fight among themselves. If they saw someone walking to their tipi that looked needy, they would shut the flap and not give hospitality. These new generations from the Second World had forgotten the stories of the below world and of Creator's sadness that turned to anger. They began to believe that they owned the gifts from Creator and did not share with their cousins.

When many moons had passed, the People of the mountains came to the People of the valley and made war on them. They stole the things most precious to the Valley People. They killed many in the tribe, forgetting that they were all brothers. It was a sad day for mothers in both villages as they buried their sons and daughters.

When a time had passed, the elders of the Valley People could hear their women grieving, so they held council. They were angry and wanted revenge. They did ceremony to Creator asking for protection and victory and then went to retrieve their things and another war broke out.

The Valley People thought Creator had not answered their prayers. But that was not true; how could Creator protect one brother from another? They were both of his heart and the beat is as one to the Great Mystery. He could only watch as the Two Leggeds began to fail at love, hospitality, and goodness.

Creator looked down in disgust at the way the Two Legged had forgotten the lessons of hospitality and generosity taught by the old ones of the Ant Tribe.

In his disgust he puffed out a deep breath on Ina Makha and suddenly she became very cold. People in the mountains and in the North began to freeze in their very steps. Many gave their spirit breath back to Creator at that moment.

Giant Ice Mountains were made where lakes had lived before. Many of the giant four-legged ones were frozen solid before they could swallow their food. This cold was so harsh even the flying ones were not spared. They fell from the cold sky on the breath of Creator and gave their spirit to the Great Mystery for safe keeping. The rich green hair froze and died from the body of Ina Makha and she shook from the cold. Many Stone People were broken in half by the giant freeze.

Rivers were frozen as they tried to flow and all creatures of land, sea, and air gave their spirit breath to Creator. Many of the Two Legged were freezing and giving up their spirit breath before they could build a fire for warmth. The sorrow and crying from First Woman and First Man echoed across the surface of Ina Makha and gave Wind a new voice of sadness.

Because Creator loved his people so much, he sent Ant to find First Man and First Woman again. When they saw their old friend from the world below, they knew this was to be the end of their Second World. They shivered and ran quickly to Hollow Tree, the one who stands over Ant's home. Even as they came near they felt themselves shrinking. First Man could no longer hold the healing crystal and had to lay it near Hollow Tree.

First Woman was crying for all her descendants who were dying in the cold on the surface. She was grieving the loss of her wonderful home and all the riches she had gathered for herself. She mourned the loss of Sister Moon's cool, soft light and Brother Sun's bright warmth.

First Man and Ant could not console her. The grief of a mother runs deep and her heart was broken. She cried out to Creator and said, "I thought we had taught our children well. They kept the ceremonies and were grateful for all your gifts. They gave honor and respect to us elders. Why have you banished us to the below world again?" she asked.

In a soft and loving song the Great Mystery spoke to her heart. "First Woman, you were a good mother and grandmother but the children and the children's children did not believe the legends because they did not hear them often enough. They could not remember the legends of the below world and so they were not of a generous and hospitable spirit. There is much more to honoring me than ceremonies. I would have honor through the hearts of all my People. When they love each other enough, there will be no wars and killing. They must learn to keep the traditions of ceremony and remember the legends from their hearts and not from the mind alone."

Creator thought words into First Woman's heart and they said, "You and First Man did not use the healing powers of Crystal so you did not stay in health and wellness. Children become the example of what the parents are. It is as the image in the lake; it can only give you back what you show to it. You must 'Walk in Beauty' to show the example."

"What is this 'Walk in Beauty' Creator?" She humbly asked.

"That is to walk the path I make for you in the foot prints I leave behind. When you follow Wolf, you move in a crouched position to see things from his level. When you follow Deer, you run swiftly in the open and hide quietly in the trees. So when you 'Walk in Beauty' you will walk as I do, in harmony and balance with all that is. You must teach the children in legend and story how it could feel to 'Walk in Beauty' and you must show them how this should look upon their hearts." First Man heard in his heart this answer as well.

When First Woman and her mate heard this, they realized that they had not been strong enough in teaching the lessons of hospitality and generosity because they had neglected their own memories of Iktomi and the Ant tribe. They did not tell stories of Worm and Stone Nation because they did not want the children to become tired of listening. They told only of their own strength and endurance as if they were the saviors of the people through some effort of their own. They forgot about the path Creator had set for them and they forgot the good friends who lived in the below world.

They had brought bones to Ant's Hollow Tree many times. When the bones were clean they used them for tool making and brought more raw bones to Hollow Tree. But they forgot that this was a generous gift to Ant and began to think of the Ant People as servants and slaves. Sometimes they had not left any meat on the bones at all, because they boiled them in soup and left no nourishment for Ant and his tribe. There even came a time when the Two Leggeds forgot the Ant Tribe and left the bones where they fell on Mother Earth. Even First Man and First Woman had forgotten the lessons of hospitality and generosity.

This is how they began a new life in the land below; more determined to learn about generosity and hospitality. They began learning the lessons and had many children. Their good friend Grandfather Ant had 'crossed the river' and they missed him. This time their host was an elder who was grandson of their old friend Grandfather Ant. They were not sure they understood this 'crossing the river' so they questioned the grandson.

He explained, "Because we are of the Creepy Crawly Tribe, we have short lives. We give our spirit breath to Creator and lay our bodies down to feed Ina Makha so she can have a long and healthy life."

"Yes that would be right, for you are the most generous ones we have ever known. You do not care who does the work; all are fed and kept safe. You blaze a trail for one another taking turns in the lead to make it easier for those who follow. You care for your young in the below world until they are strong enough to travel to the surface and take their place in your working army" said First Man.

First Woman spoke in a humbled voice, having

forgotten her grief for a while. "I wish we had taught our children as well as you have yours, for they might still be alive had we been stronger."

"This was a hard lesson for you, but like my Grandfather before me, I welcome you to our land and we will help you learn many more things. Let us hope your new descendants will know the legends are taught from a place of truth. No story or legend is too small for they hold the lessons of our people and wisdoms of our elders," said Grandson Ant.

"You will need to listen to the historians of Ina Makha, the Stone Tribe, for they have wisdoms we cannot possibly understand" Grandson Ant added.

The truth about the lessons available to them was like a blinding light in the hearts of First Man and his mate. They would be open and willing to learn from the Stone Tribe and all others from the world below. They would remember to tell the stories more often and to teach the children and the children's children to tell the legends.

First Man and First Woman began teaching the new generations about the land on the surface. These stories were hard to believe, as this generation had never seen the surface. First Man realized he must be strong and make his children listen to the wisdom and the teaching in the legends. He and First Woman spent many hours teaching ceremonies and reminding everyone to honor and respect Creator. They taught them about gratitude and how to be hospitable and generous. They gave small stones to the children to help them remember the legends.

They helped the children fashion little pouches to hold the stones that would hang close to their hearts. These stones were smaller than a grain of sand as the people were small as Ant but the power of these little stones was felt by all.

Many children and children's children until the seventh generation were born and they were taught the lessons by the elders through legends and stories.

Again, the Stone Tribe told First Man "We will record this great freeze on our bodies so you can remember that your children destroyed Ina Makha with their cold hearts filled with greed and killing."

First Man was grateful for this recording and promised to show the signs to his children and his children's children if ever they were returned to the surface. This was the Second World destroyed by the two-legged and First Man wondered how much Creator would take before he and First Woman were destroyed and then no People would breathe on Ina Makha.

First Man began to show hospitality to all who came his way. He would give them his food or his blanket and on some days when it seemed he had nothing, he would give them love, acceptance and a well-told story. He always had stories and legends to share that carried wise teachings for those who could hear. He showed his children and the children's children how to give a gift of hair or fingernail to Mother Earth before they picked up any gifts she was offering. Many times First Woman would invite all who could come to sit with her in ceremony.

They both spoke of Creator and His great abundance. They told stories of Iktomi and Worm and even Grandfather Ant. Everyone would laugh and feel happy when Grandson Ant would humbly bow his head while First Man bragged about his generosity.

It was after many generations that Grandson Ant came to First Man and said "It is time to return to the surface; Creator is calling you."

The people were very excited for they knew the stories and legends taught by First Man, the grandfather of all people. They were very generous and before they left on the trail to the surface, they ran around making gifts of all their possessions to the Ant Tribe, as a way to say thank you for keeping them safe. No one was frightened and no one was selfish.

First Woman smiled and said to First Man "We have done well in our teachings. These children know how to honor, respect, and be grateful to Creator and they are very generous and hospitable. They will live in this way even after they reach the surface." First Man smiled for he could see it was true.

However he had forgotten about the small pouches holding the medicine of the Stone Tribe being too small for the children to see once they arrived on the surface.

When they reached a certain place on the trail to the surface, Grandson Ant said, "I am old and tired. You know the way from here. You are already beginning to grow to your full size again. Thank you for being our guests and helping with our work. Please remember to be generous with the bones you leave and do not think we are here only to serve you."

In humbleness and gratitude, First Woman touched Grandson Ant's face and told him, "We could never forget our old friend your Grandfather or his grandson and in his honor and yours, we will provide well for you. Thank you for everything." She turned with a touch of sadness on her face for the missing of her Ant family and followed her mate to the surface.

Again it was full moon when they arrived on the surface and First Man looked back to the Stone People. First Man knew this was the Third World. When First Man looked back, there was Crystal, the one gifted to him so long ago and beside her lay a Flat Black stone with cracks and lines etched on his face, but tumbled smooth by the grinding powers of Ina Makha as the ice melted away.

"What is this about?" asked First Man.

"This stone is to remind you that the lives of many were taken when your tribe lost its way in the world before this. We were all given a world of perfect beauty but because you forgot to be grateful and love each other, it was destroyed by earthquakes and volcanoes and many died," said the Stone Elder.

"Then we were given a Second World, perfect in every way, but because of your cold hearts filled with fear, greed and selfishness with a lack of hospitality, it was destroyed by Creator's cold freezing breath," Stone Elder clicked his voice on the nearby Stone People.

"Now we walk in this Third World that is perfect in every way. Carry these stones so you will remember all that has happened. We are your historians; we hold the memories of all the past worlds. Keep us sacred," said the Eldest of all Stone People. He was and still is the most ancient of all, for it was he that was born on the day Ina Makha was made.

First Man knew the wisdom of this Ancient One. First Man gave the smooth stone with the cracks and lines showing through it, the name of Wisdom and put the stone in a pouch around his neck. Wisdom would remind him that Ina Makha is sacred and to destroy her is murder. He carried the stones close to his heart, in what he now called a medicine pouch, to remind him to be honorable, respectful, generous and hospitable as well as a brave and peaceful provider.

First Man and his mate were grateful for all the lessons they had learned and for the legends that had taught their children and their children's children. They walked together towards Sister Moon.

First Man was trying to remember that he needed to teach all the generations about the medicine pouches and how to fill them with stones. He was so excited about the new world and the perfection of Ina Makha that he decided to tell everyone about it later when they were settled in their new village.

The people were greeted with soft and cool light. Many walked in awe as they looked at the Standing Tall Ones and the lush hair on Ina Makha's body. Some could hear songs from Wolf and Coyote welcoming them home. Some heard Owl speak about remembering, from his wisdom place.

All the People were filled with gratitude.

Many of the young men came to First Man and said, "We wish to build a fire like you described, for we have never seen its flaming glory."

First Man was pleased that they remembered the legend of Fire, for it was a sign that they had listened well to his stories. He taught them to make fire and to thank the Standing Tall Tribe for its wood and the dried Grass Tribe for feeding fire.

First Woman gathered sacred sage in the moon light and taught the daughters how to smudge one another for purification.

A feast was held with much dancing and singing around the fire. As Dawn began calling, they turned East and held a ceremony of gratitude for this new day and this new life.

Many went to live where their ancestors had lived. They had listened to the legends from First Man telling of the lands where their ancestors had been and they learned the paths to reach these faraway places. They would be wiser than the ones before them.

They would use this new knowledge to protect themselves from making the old mistakes. Before they went separate ways, they taught each other to speak with their hands. This was done so if they began to speak in different languages as their fathers and grandfathers of old had done, that they could always talk to one another and not fight. With this hand language, they could speak and understand, brother to brother. This sign language works among all men to this day, even those who have no sound in their ears.

Many generations were born and Creator was pleased with all that the two-legged had learned from Ant Tribe during their time in the below world. There was no fear in the hearts of the people when they came to the surface, because

First Man and First Woman had told many stories. They had learned of love and goodness and about Creator. All the People loved Him and honored Him with prayers and ceremonies of gratitude because they remembered the legends.

The Generations were living in peace and harmony for many moons. The ceremonies held for honor, respect, gratitude, and generosity were pleasing to Creator. He saw the hospitality of the People as they welcomed all who traveled near them. Great Mystery was happy with the legends and stories being shared around many fires. All beings of Ina Makha were at peace and enjoyed abundance from Creator's blessings.

As the generations continued, the elders taught well the lessons they had learned. The People knew how to be grateful to Creator and approach him in humble respect through ceremony and ritual from traditions passed down in the stories and legends. They grew in love and peace with their families.

Then one day, First Man learned how to ride Horse and he could travel for many days without rest. Horse was happy to make this gift to the Two Legged so they could hunt easier and travel long distances to see family. Unfortunately, people fear what they do not know and, as happens with Two Leggeds, things could not be perfect for too long.

Some Two Leggeds had gone to the Mountains, a place of long winters, and became very pale so they looked nearly white. While some, who had gone to the southern deserts, were now warmed by Sun until they looked toasted brown and nearly black. Some had gone to secret places in the East and had to squint as they walked towards Sun's eastern dawn. Their eyes began to stay that way and they gleamed yellow from the kiss of Dawn Sun. There were still people of red skin who had stayed in the West near Hollow Tree to provide bones for the Ant Tribe. These People were all still brothers and cousins but they had begun to look very different in each other's eyes.

With Horse as their guide, the People traveled to new lands and met these people of different colors. Since some people of a particular color were afraid of these strangers who rode Horse and looked different, they were not hospitable. They had decided that it was only necessary to practice the wisdoms of hospitality with their own kind. They did not see the strangers as family but as intruders.

It mattered not who the traveler was, be he black from the South traveling to the pale white ones of the North or the yellow ones from the East coming to the red ones of the West. It was always the same. Fear of the strangeness would cause hearts to shut. The language of the hands was not used by many as they could only see the differences. They did not love one another as brothers, but rather they feared one another as enemies. They had no legends to teach them about the colors and so they were not accepting of one another.

Creator was worried as he watched his children begin to fight about who should live where and who had the correct skin color. He saw them argue over who was more important in the eyes of Creator Himself.

How could they not know He had made them all, He wondered? He was sad about the few who seemed filled with anger and madness and spoke often of the war times. Creator knew that if they thought about this long enough, they would go to war again. When the Two Legged thinks long on a thing, they make it happen. Again, talk of war and hatred filled the air and before long, brother stood against brother, forgetting all the lessons they had been taught.

In only a few short years after this time, the wars began. The People forgot to be honorable and humble; they forgot about gratitude. Hospitality was traded for hostility and everywhere, the people were not in ceremony but rather they were in forgetfulness.

First Man and First Woman tried to warn them. They stood on the highest mountain peaks and called down to the children of all colors telling them they were a beautiful rainbow of color to Creator and that he loved them all equally. First Woman begged her children to stop fighting and to offer ceremony of gratitude and respect to Creator. She called on them to welcome their brothers of every color in hospitality and not to be fearful.

But all these warnings went unheeded and the generations fought for supremacy and forgot the Good Medicine Way they had been taught. Creator was saddened by all the pain and lack of love in the world.

He talked with Ina Makha and said, "We must start again, Mother of all. This time we must give them the most powerful lesson."

Ina Makha knew how it pained Great Mystery, most Wakhan of all beings, to once again bring destruction on her body. She watched him weep and felt his tears fill her canyons and cover even her mountains. This brought more sadness to Creator and he shed tears all the more.

Soon, the only thing not covered by water was Hollow Tree and First Man and First Woman who stood there shrinking to the size of Ant once more. Just as Creator's last tear fell, First Man lay down the stones he had carried in his medicine pouch for so many generations and stepped on the path to the below world.

In a few steps, he was not surprised to see an unknown member of the great Ant Tribe coming up the path to him. First Man stopped and with his arm still supporting his grieving wife, he bowed his head and asked for sanctuary with his Ant cousins.

"I am the son of the ancestors who have helped you in other worlds and I welcome you to our village," said this kind and honorable Ant.

First Woman would not be comforted and her tears fell for many moons. When Creator could not stand to hear her weep anymore, He called out to her "First Woman, mate of First Man come talk with me."

First Woman was surprised to hear the song of Creator's heart. She looked in the darkness of the below world but could not see from where the song came. She lifted her voice and said "Oh mighty Wakhan Tunkasila, how much more must I endure?"

Creator knew how hard it had been for her to watch her children and her children's children die. He understood her pain and wanted to help her see what her duty must be. He whispered between the stones, "Sit quietly and listen, for I will make a promise to you, First Woman."

First Woman humbly sank to the ground. She wanted to smudge herself in sage smoke to be fit and clean before her Creator, but there is no fire in the below world and no sage grows there. She could hear the drum beat of Creator's heart and heard his wind song. He promised her that all the knowledge that could save her children would be given to her, and that she would remember it this time. He promised that she could tell all the stories and legends with no hesitation and that she would be an even better mother this time.

He showed her how to braid her long hair from three equal parts. He explained that as long as He was the first strand and the people were the second strand and she could be the third strand that they would be strong and powerful in this new form of unity.

She listened closely and her tears began to subside. She had hoped to never give birth again. She was old and tired and did not want to lose more children. She thought if she avoided her mate and bore no more children, she could be free from this grief and loss.

She began to realize, as she listened to her most sacred Creator that it would not be possible to close herself off from all love and stay in this misery forever. She knew it was her job to follow the Red Road that Creator placed before her feet and not question his plan. So she rose from the ground, dried her tears, stroked her new braids, and put her foot on the path Creator provided.

She was thinking that she was tired and growing old and wondered why she had not just stayed above to die with her children.

Creator answered her unasked question. "First Woman, I will give you a new wisdom. You will become the Grandmother of all who live and you will teach a new harmony and balance to your children."

First Woman called to First Man that he might be strengthened by Creator's words as well. "Come quick and listen to our most honored Wakhan Tunkasila (sacred grandfather). He has promised us wisdom," she cried out.

When First Man joined her, they sat with heads humbly bowed and waited to hear from Creator. He came singing a new legend for them. In this legend, he told of a place where he lived in a peaceful and contented land. A place where all the children and all the generations they had brought forth still lived on. This sacred place was 'across the great river' and had no wars, no sadness, no tears and everything is remembered. It is the place of perfection, for that is where Creator lives.

They could not imagine such a place and were shocked to hear that all the people ever born had not died, but only moved to a new land 'across the river'.

Creator explained further by telling them "How could I take back the spirit breath? Can you breathe the breath you last took? I would not want to destroy that spirit breath, as it came from my heart and was unique to each of the children who lived and then died."

"How is it, oh Great Mystery that we have never been able to go to this land of no sadness? Why must we continue to live without our people and always make new generations?" asked First Man.

"I have known all things from before you were created and all things after. I knew you would make many mistakes and destroy Ina Makha many times. I needed you to stay alive and learn so you could build on these lessons and gain wisdom from one world to the next," He answered.

"Will we ever be able to go to this place 'across the river'?" asked First Woman.

"In the next world, you will be allowed to 'Cross the River'. For after that world, there will be only three more. Those three must stay in mystery until their time is made ready," He said as he gave them the knowledge of eternity.

Now they knew the spirit would never die but the body could be left on this side of the river. They knew they had much to learn about other things while they were here again with the Stone Tribe and the Ant People in the below world.

To have this knowledge and the ability to teach it was a powerful gift. They would share this with each other many times to make a legend from it and again have children. When First Man heard of this, with joy in his heart, he began a ceremony of gratitude and humility to Creator.

First Woman spoke from her place of new knowledge and deeper wisdom. "Listen, my husband no longer will we do ceremony. Now, we will become ceremony" She said.

"How can that be, wife?" asked First Man.

"We will *be* the ceremony when we dance and when we drum. We will *be* ceremony when our songs and prayers reach Creator's ears. We can never forget the ceremonies if we *are* the ceremonies." She said.

First Man thought for a moment and said, "Yes, I can see the truth of your words. We must choose how to teach our children before we bring them to this life. Where will we learn this wisdom?" He asked.

"We must talk to the historians, the Stone Tribe, for they know all the past and how to keep it sacred" she said.

Then she added from her new wisdom place, "We will have dreams and visions where Creator will teach us how to always walk in spirit and in harmony. We will be with Ina Makha as ceremony and not as her ruler. We will *become* the ceremony that pleases Creator and nurtures our Mother Earth"

First Man and First Woman went to the Stone Tribe and asked how they should teach the children who would come to this world. The Stone People offered their wisdom by explaining that everyone has a path to walk in Creator's plan They explained that the path of the Two Leggeds is to *be* ceremony for His pleasure. They were beginning to understand.

One of the elder stones spoke in a gravelly old voice and said "It is easy for you to be ceremony. Remember when Creator looks to find the sweet smell of sage, sweet grass or cedar, He sees who is offering it. He sees the smoke and prayer offering as a part of the one He is watching. It is all one thing for Him. He feels your heartbeat as your drum calls and your feet dance. He knows the songs you sing to Him are on the winds of your spirit breath and, as one, you come to His ears."

First Man said "Yes, and when we use the sacred tobacco and offer Chanupa (pipe ceremony), we will come to Creator as pure and perfect smoke. Now I see how we can *become* ceremony."

First Woman said to Stone Elder "Thank you for your wisdom. We will never forget this and all the children from now on will know they *are* the ceremony. They are the ones Creator loves, so of course, they are the ceremony He seeks."

Then they wondered about this thing called vision and the one known as dreams. They knew it was time to meet with other wisdom keepers of the below world. First Man and First Woman took this new knowledge and put it in their hearts.

Then they went to No Eyes, their friend of the worm tribe and asked him for help in learning new wisdom. "You have been in the blind, in the land of the below for all your generations. How have you managed to stay happy with no arms or legs? Why have you never gone to war with one another?" they asked.

"This is an easy question," said the old Grandfather Worm. "My name is No Eyes, because I do not need them. All of my people know that if we fight, we may break our enemy in half and in so doing, we make two enemies, for both halves will live. We know that if we are selfish and eat too much, we could grow so fast that we then cannot fit down our hole and we would dry out and die in the Sun and Wind. So being generous saves our lives. We know if we are not humble and crawl on our bellies as intended, we will have no method of travel. Because we are not troubled with sight, we see no difference in one another. We only know alikeness. We share our hospitality. On long winter nights, we survive by being entwined one with another until we are a giant warm ball where all are safe."

"How do you know this is true, No Eyes?" asked First Man.

"Because we see through visions and dreams rather than eyes," he said.

No Eyes continued, "We know the way of our path. There are pictures in our hearts and our mind's eye that are full of lessons. When we look into these visions and dreams, we see the lessons we should learn and the ones we should teach. Creator has given us these invisible pictures so that we might each learn directly from His heart. You cannot see my vision or my dream but you can be told of it. I can help you see and learn your dream lessons by asking you questions and you can help me see my visions more clearly when you ask questions of me."

"I am not sure I understand," said First Woman. "What questions should I ask you?"

"If I offer to tell you my dream, it will seem as an unfinished legend or story. You will want more information so you will ask me to explain better. Then I will hear my own words and it will become clearer to me what my lesson is about."

"These are very wise thoughts," said First Woman. "We must make a legend about this so the children will remember these true things."

She began thinking of how to tell her children that it would be better to have no legs than to forget how to bend down on the knees in prayer. It would be better to have no eyes than to judge their brothers by the way they look. It would be better to have no hands and arms than to take from others. They needed to know that making war would only create more enemies. They must be taught that selfishness will destroy them and only through hospitality and generosity will they survive. They needed to hear about this magic dream time and vision place so they would hear Creator's voice through the invisible pictures.

First Man then spoke to Young Ant who was the son of his old friend's son.

"I have been a guest of your land many times and each time, you teach us many new things. Can you tell me what you think is the most important of these lessons?"

Young Ant tipped his head to one side, as all ants are prone to do, and he said

"You have seen us make a path for those who follow and how that makes it easier for everyone. What you do not see is that the path makers are the elders. The elders are the ones who put the path in order and they are the ones teaching those who follow how to walk this path."

"Yes I see what you mean, Young Ant" said First Man. "And how do you learn to work so well together?" he asked.

"We each have a job that is special to us. This is so each of us feels happy about ourselves. We have learned from our fathers who learned from their fathers that each ant is precious to Creator. We know all jobs are equal. Who would be happier, a man with food and no home or the man with a home and no food?" asked Young Ant. "You see, we realize that the tribe must be united to survive for we need food gatherers and builders alike" He continued.

"Oh" said First Woman. "I see there is no jealousy or selfishness, for it is the combination of workers that make the tribe strong."

"Yes" said Young Ant, "and all that we do is in honor and respect for our brothers and that is how we show our love to Creator; through our cooperation. It is Creator who made us and it is He that keeps us together. All that we do for ourselves and for our tribe is what we do to show gratitude to our Creator."

First Woman began to make braids in her hair as Creator had shown her and said, "These braids will, from now on, represent unity so we never forget to teach the children this lesson."

As she divided her hair into three sections, she said, "This first section is for Creator and I add the next section for our Tribe, and to that, the last section I add is for me. This makes a braid of all the parts to balance us in harmony with Creator's plan for our unity."

First Man had watched all this and saw the wisdom. He realized that the story of the braid and the legend of No Eyes the worm, along with the story from Stone about *becoming* ceremony, were the very things Creator wanted them to remember. This was truly wisdom. They would be teaching the children about all these lessons in the stories and legends they would imagine during dream and vision time.

The truth of being ceremony, of working together in harmony and non-judgment, in generosity and hospitality and, most of all, respecting and honoring Creator through unity would be the legends for his children.

First Woman said to First Man "I think maybe there is more we need to know before we bring any children to this world but I am not sure what that is." Because her heart was true, Creator spoke though her husband's voice.

"You are an honorable mother, First Woman, so this is what you need to know. The love you feel covering you now is most sacred and it comes from your Creator. You must learn to love one another with all your hearts in that same Sacred Love. Always be forgiving and hold only love in your heart for Mitakuye Oyasin." He said.

"Yes" said First Woman. "The most important of all is love."

So they brought forth more children and their children brought children. They had love and compassion for each other and they were respectful and non-judgmental. They were generous and humble in their hospitality. They became ceremony every day to dance with Creator in His heart. As they braided their hair each morning, they remembered the unity song;

"First Creator,
Then my Tribe,
Followed by me,
Makes unity"

They started to remember their night dreams and to see day visions. They were leaning to communicate with Creator. They were learning that many answers to their prayers were hidden in these dreams and visions. They were learning to listen to Creator in this way.

The generations moved throughout the land of Ant and they worked hard to help in all ways they could. Each felt good about himself because he was loved by the next. The harmony and balance among the People had never been so strong. When the generations had reached the seventh generation, Creator called First Man and First Woman.

"You have done well these long many years. I am proud of all you have learned and how you have taught it to your children. Using symbols like your braid to remind them of wisdom through unity and making more stories and legends so you can pass on your history is a gift you should be very proud of. The way you have learned to be ceremony and how you are teaching your children makes my heart glad," He said.

The Ant Tribe began circling around the elders and singing the song of honor. They had a gift for the people and wished to share it while they were in the glow of Creator's words. They brought out an outfit for First Woman and one for First Man. They were of the softest doe skin and had many beautiful designs painted on them from the root dyes they made. Fringe hung long on both outfits and feathers of humming bird had been cut down to fit on a tiny staff. These outfits were gifted to the elders with words of wisdom from the Ant Tribe's leader.

Looking in the eyes of First Man and First Woman, their friend Young Ant said, "When you came here, I was Young Ant and now I am a Grandfather. We are about to say good-by to our Two Legged friends again. Our tribe chose to honor you with these outfits so you could teach your children and children's children to dress in this manner. You can take pride and respect in yourselves for working together to keep peace and harmony on the land. You will 'walk in beauty' in this fine regalia for all your generations. You will dance before leaders and beggars alike. You will lead in the ceremonies you become wherever you travel. You will be respected and loved by many nations. There will be jealousy and fear from some who meet you on this path but, in the end, you will lead them all to Creator's great feast. You have been given directions about how to 'cross the river' when your work is finished and you will meet the many generations waiting there for you. This is your gift because you will bring love for Mitakuye Oyasin (All my Relations) to Ina Makha. Travel well your path, my friends, and remember your Ant cousins."

"Thank you again for all your hospitality and we will bless this lodge, standing under Hollow Tree, with many meaty bones from now on" said First Man.

First Woman looked at all her new sisters in the Ant

tribe and she was thankful for the way they taught her to love. She beamed at her children and their children's children as she turned to follow First Man up the trail to the surface path.

Iktomi (spider) stood by the opening in Hollow Tree, waiting to speak with First Man and First Woman. As they came near, they could feel the eyes of Iktomi looking into their hearts. First Man stopped and lowered his eyes in humbleness as he waited for Iktomi to speak.

"Do you recall my advice about weaving a web to hold your family together?" asked Iktomi.

"Yes, but I think I did not understand" answered First Man.

"You must become ceremonies that unite every tribe. You need to see the heart of every being and not only the outside skin they wear. When the hand language is used, it should be eloquent and gentle for others to read. There must be places on Mother Earth that are held Sacred. All land is Sacred, but some places are more special. There must be a time of gathering the harvest and preserving it for winter, and this is also true for the love in your hearts. You must harvest love and then re-plant the seeds of love to keep it growing" said Iktomi.

First Woman raised her eyes to look into Iktomi's face and she asked in a small voice "How can we always have love, when anger and resentment and even greed lives in the minds of Two Leggeds?" she asked.

"By remembering, that it is in the mind, not the heart, where these not so pleasant feelings live" Iktomi answered. "The mind is a powerful gift and can be used to discover many things, but it has not the tenderness and wisdom of the heart. The heart beats in unison with Creator. The heart is always fragile and will not carry fear or anger because it would break under such a heavy burden. The mind is strong and can hold much resentment, anger, fear, and greed. The mind has a master and it is the heart. The Heart must be what leads your mind. If I walk on my delicate web with heavy steps of stomping anger, it would surely break. But if I am light as air and use my faith, love, and goodness in each step, the web becomes stronger."

"I think I am beginning to understand," said First Woman. "I must show our children how to speak little and listen much, how to walk in humbleness and not arrogance. There should only be softness in our steps if we are to care for Mother Earth and not just take from her body."

"When all Two Leggeds hold these beliefs in their heart, they will only pick up the Stone People for wellness and never for weapons," said First Man.

"Yes my friends, you are leaving our below world with much wisdom. I hope you enjoy the Fourth World, as it is the one of final choice. It is the one that will let you choose the path of Two Leggeds for the balance of eternity," said Iktomi.

First Man touched the surface of Fourth World and turned to find his old friends Crystal and Wisdom. They waited for him with a pile of Lava Stone and smooth Ocean, Lake and River stone. One was a mountain stone with an image of snail on its face.

First Man could remember that Crystal came to him after the mighty shifts and volcanoes of First World holding fire pictures in her heart. He knew Wisdom had joined him after the freezing cold had destroyed Second World. Now he looked at the little snail in mountain stone and knew this was his gift from the Third World that had been buried in water. He knew he had much to learn about Lava and Ocean, as they were the healing stones.

First Man would not let the others come to the surface until he knew more about these gifts. He was taught in an instant knowing!

Lava would be for the sacred cleansing at Inipi Ceremony, called "Sweat Lodge" by some. He was shown Inyan Pejuta "Stone Medicine" from the smooth Ocean,

River, and Lake Stone. When He held this knowledge in his heart, he picked up the sacred stones and placed them in a bundle over his shoulder. These Stone People had much to share with all the generations. As First Man was ready to leave, his eyes fell on a beautiful rainbow hidden in a black stone.

Creator whispered in his ear "First Man, take this rainbow stone and hold it to your heart. It is a reminder that I will paint often in the sky. This rainbow will be the picture of my promise to you, that I will never destroy your world with water again. It is to remind you that I am with you always and you can love as I love if you keep your heart open."

First Man then turned and motioned with the hand language and all the people followed First Woman to his side. When all the two-leggeds stood in Sister Full Moon's light, they became a bright and blissful ceremony.

Even the Star Tribe could see the difference. They knew that the understanding of love was going to have a powerful influence on the Two Leggeds. All the flying ones and the Swimming Ones were turning loops in joyful fun. Even Otter joined in the flips of happiness as they felt a new awakening coming to the People. All the Four Legged and Creepy Crawlies joined the Standing Tall Ones and the Rooted Ones in a dance of glory for they too felt that love had transformed the People.

From this joy came the true understanding behind the name for all beings that carry the spirit breath of Creator. This name is Mitakuye Oyasin and it means 'All my Relations', which is the Mother Earth tribe, so we must care for all of her and all of her living beings if Two Legged ones are to survive. This shows that People are related to every living thing because we all have the same spirit breath. We are not blessed more than No Eyes of the Worm Tribe and not less than the coldest Stone, for Creator is pleased with all His work. He does not make things unworthy of His love. He is Love so He can only make things of goodness and righteousness.

"Mitakuye Oyasin", sang all the People, for they knew Creator was with them. They had remembered this name from the underworld and they brought it to the surface with love for all living things.

Creator boomed in His thunder voice. How proud He felt of First Man and First Woman and all their children.

He said, "You are on the edge of the canyon wall. You can be lifted by the breeze to higher places than ever you could imagine if you keep your heads up and walk in harmony. You can hang your heads in shame and sadness over wars you might create and fall over the edge of 'Canyon with No Bottom'. You have a great choice to make. I have brought you to this Fourth World with knowledge of all things here and the wisdom of Now. You also have a forgotten knowledge of what has always been and what will come."

Creator knew some among the People would be prophets and tell of great awakenings in spirit. He knew that the healing they would learn were medicines not even thought of before. He knew trouble would settle on the people again but that this time, some would know the truth and stand by it.

This was a time when man would learn to make canoes and fish traps and snares of all kinds. All the People would learn about tools and they would grow in knowledge. He knew Iktomi's web would carry the words of the People across the great Oceans and the People of all colors would still be brothers.

He also knew that one day the Kachina would walk a headless path, one behind the other, and fall into the sea. This would be a sign to the people that they could be in power and make a choice. They could decide to live in harmony and ever growing spirituality or they could again harm one another and Ina Makha.

With new knowledge came the ability to listen.

Crystal taught the Two Leggeds to harness her power and use it to magnify other powers that she would work with in harmony.

Diamond gave his sharp and hardy edge to the people for tools and for hearing things better. Lava ground himself to powder and made the red clays for the Red People.

Granite and others joined to pave the paths the People used for their fast horses made of metals from the Stone Tribe.

When People began to see Stone's ability, they invited the Stone People to make jewelry of their gems and to make medicines from their bodies. The Stone People became companions with one another in combinations they had never held before. They could be cement if lime of one stone joined clay and sand of still other stones.

In this new world of lodges that are bigger than the Standing Tall Ones, where metal Winged Ones fly in Sky Nation, many gifts for the people will be born from the gifts of the Stone Tribe. Mechanical beasts will dig into Ina Makha's breast and take many of the Stone Tribe for heat and for building and for making dams on her mighty waters. The Stone Tribe gives the gifts to the People to use them with honor.

Creator gave the people the power of decision, free will and choice, because they now have all the knowledge of man. It is up to the people to live in the manner most pleasing to Creator. We live in this world now; the world of free will and free choice.

This Fourth World has changed much since First Man and First Woman came to the surface. One change, that has been a blessing to all, has been death. Creator provided a way for us to join Him 'Across the Great River' in only a few years. Now, we do not live until the seventh generations. We are still responsible for passing on the best we can to all and protect Mother Earth for the seventh generation, but we will no longer live forever.

Finally, First Man and First Woman became 'Ceremony for Crossing the River'. They were blessed to join Creator in His mystery home where all their generations live. They dance in Sky each night with pleasure at our growth and they weep in forests over much of the destruction of Ina Makha. Now that we are waking up to our paths, we must make it easier for others to follow.

The path over greed and around selfishness is just under the mountain of bigotry. If you turn right past hatred and up the trail to Love, you will see the joy of Creator near the end of the road. Someday, we will be able to meet First Man and First Woman, as they are our ancestors. Let us all live for the awakening of this world as we plan to become our own 'Crossing the River Ceremony'.
Ah Ho

Hollow Bone Legend

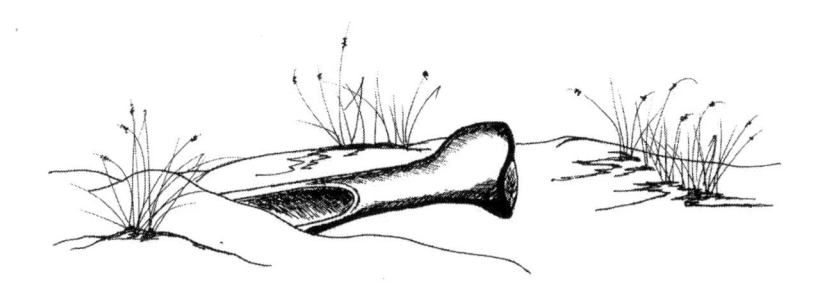

In the traditional Native American way we strive to be what we call the 'Hollow Bone'. This is how we describe our ability to allow Creator's Spirit to work through us. Imagine a dried and sun bleached, Buffalo leg-bone made of calcium. It appears hard as a rock and in some ways totally useless. In the Native belief when we see ourselves as this Hollow Bone we see that in and of ourselves, we are useless. It is only when we are filled with the Spirit of Creator that we have great value and merit.

We believe that if we can be this conduit, this 'Hollow Bone', then the purity of love and compassion from Creator will flow through us. As long as we keep ego, selfishness, self-centeredness, greed or other negative aspects of human behavior out of the Hollow Bone we can serve as the open-ended vessel for Creator's blessings to flow freely.

We believe that our task in life is to stay as free as possible from the things of the mind that would restrict the flow of Creator's gifts. It is our belief that if we are humble and grateful with no ulterior motives that Creator will work through us to assist all of the living beings on Mother Earth. This belief is similarly stated in the Bible when we are told to let our light shine for others to see and not hide it under a bush.

Of course no one can maintain this perfect balance at all times. We all have challenges in life that cause us to lose our way from time to time. The goal of this legend is to *remind ourselves to return to balance.*

Some Native people believe that when we are working with the Spirit of Creator, we simply need to be open and clear about our intentions. We focus on letting go of personal weaknesses and pray for strength and guidance.

This is a balanced perspective for many who work in the healing arts. If we think that we must 'heal' an illness every time we touch a client then we have filled the Hollow Bone with ego. It is not up to us to 'heal' anyone. The outcome is always up to Creator. There might be reasons we do not understand for illness, pain, and disease in another individual. As the Hollow Bone we have only the right to 'seek' Creator's gifts of wellness for ourselves or another person, but we do not have the right to 'expect' the results to be wellness. The results are up to Creator. If we take credit for the ones who are healed then we must take blame for those who are not. It is much easier to give all credit to Creator and remain the Hollow Bone.

Most Native people believe we have the responsibility to be grateful for the wellness we witness and nothing more. Giving all credit to Creator and taking none for ourselves will insure that we remain humble. If we are filled with ego and a desire to become a gifted healer, we are setting ourselves up for a difficult life. As a Hollow Bone we simply act as a conduit to serve in the way Creator wishes. We are instructed to love one another, to serve one another and to live in harmony. These beliefs are demonstrated in many spiritual practices around the world.

There is no risk of us contracting the pain from the client/patient as the energy can only move in one direction. The negative or unbalanced energy that leaves the client/patient is like food for Mother Earth. She feeds on the waste of many beings. The droppings of animals, dead plants, dead bodies, and negative thoughts are her fertilizer. She needs the things we are finished with in order to be replenished. Our exhaled breath helps feed the plants. When we allow the Creator to flow through us with His purifying energy, we passively feed Mother Earth. This wonderful synergistic way of clearing out what is not needed from us and passing it on to Mother Earth is a perfect example of Creator's plan for balance and harmony.

Every legend told, in the oral traditions of Native Americans, is protected by the linage that passes it on. This means that each family may have a slightly different way of telling a story or that emphasis might be on specific lessons within the legend. All traditions, ceremonial descriptions and legends in this text, are from the Chas Thompson linage. In the Hollow Bone legend we can see how the individual 'becomes' a Hollow Bone and what 'medicines' of Buffalo can be received or passed on to others.

Like many legends this one can be expanded and elongated for hours of telling around the campfire (as I learned it from my father) or it can be a brief story to offer a lesson to someone who is out of balance.

Our legend goes something like this:

There was an ancient time, a time long ago, before time was in a box when there were no clocks! Sun and Moon gave us the brightness or the darkness as they were guided by Creator. Day and night served the people, for the Sky Nation knew how to provide a time for rest and a time for work. The seasons learned to follow each other to remind us of the harmony we can choose for our life. Waters were fed by melting snow caps and pure food grew in rich clean soil. The air was so clear and fresh it had the smell of fresh rain on dry dirt. Mother Earth was happy in her ancient times when men were few and their footsteps were light. It was in this time that a famous medicine man lived. He was called Wakhan Wichasa, with means Sacred or Holy Man.

Wakhan Wichasa walked the hills and valleys from village to village offering his healing herbs and gifts of wisdom to those in need of wellness. He was so humble he never asked for payment for his medicine, but said, "It is not me who brings wellness, only Creator can do that. I am only a Hollow Bone who is the tool."

He climbed the mountains and walked the ridges looking for special herbs, roots, mosses, and minerals at each elevation. He combed the sea shores and river banks where various medicines can grow. He helped with the harvest of Buffalo, Deer, Elk, and Salmon so he could gather the organs for special medicines. He had many pouches of dried roots, ground berries, or seeds that hung from his belt. With each step he took he thanked Creator for the power of his legs to carry him forward.

Wakhan Wichasa knew he was planting the seeds for the next generation as he walked. He would see his leather leggings stir up the seed pods and as they settled to the earth he blessed them with his gratitude prayers so they might grow for the next harvest. He knew many ways to pray for wellness and he was happy to *'become'* the ceremonies for his people. He was never lonely as he journeyed this solitary path because he spoke to the animals and the growing ones as his friends. He prayed continually for the people.

The people of many villages were pleased to call him their Medicine Man. The years passed and as he grew older he began to visit with worry. This had never happened to him before. He trusted that Creator would always provide for his needs. He began to think of the ones who had taught him the Good Medicine Ways. When they were elders and began to Cross the River, he felt safe in his knowledge and training. Then came a day when he thought he was the last living one with this knowledge.

When it dawned on him that he must find an apprentice and train them in the Good Medicine Ways, he began to worry. What would happen to the Good Medicine Way, if he could not find the one person, who was ready to learn? Why had he not settled with a wife and had children to train? What could he do to pass on the wisdom of the rooted ones and the stone ones to the next generation? This was not a way to walk in balance so he thought it was Creator prompting him to change his direction. It was time for him to find another to train in the Good Medicine Way.

He asked many young men in each village if they were ready to learn of the Good Medicine Ways. Some told him they were destined to be great hunters, while others said they were warriors. Some told him they were training to be spiritual leaders, fishermen or flute makers. Some were learning to be fathers and helping their children to be good providers. Wakhan Wichasa had traveled the length of the valley and over the ridge to the next valley, visiting every village and always asking who would follow him on this Good Medicine Path.

As time went by his legs became old and withered. He saw how thin and frail they had become. He went to the clear Looking Pool and saw his reflection in the water. The face of an old man peeked back at him. Was it true that he was growing so old he might not be able to visit every village? He made a small fire and offered tobacco and sage to the flames. He let his prayers flow up to Creator on the sweet smelling smoke. He asked for guidance and prayed that his body would last long enough for him to speak of these ways to another.

He knew to watch for signs from nature to receive his answers. He expected Eagle to fly high overhead and guide him to the place where he could find the next Wakhan Wichasa. But Eagle did not come. He watched to see if Deer would lead the way along a path to the one he should meet. But Deer was happy to rest under the trees in tall grass all day or wander to the river for a drink. He watched for Wolf and hoped he would sing a song that might help him locate the one who would be ready to learn the ways. But Wolf was silent.

One night as he lay his head on the sweet soil of

Mother Earth he asked Creator to send him a dream that would lead him to the right person. As he drifted off he thought he heard a group of magpies chatting away in the distance. He snapped himself awake and looked in the direction of the sound, but it was not an answer from his noisy cousin, only a trick of his old ears hearing things. Wakhan Wichasa settled in for the night with faith that Creator would answer in His own time and in His own way.

The next morning Wakhan Wichasa felt refreshed and strong so he went to the water of Looking Pool for a drink and a chat with himself. "You old fool how could you be so arrogant as to think you could wait till death was at your door to find one from the next generation? There was the woman who asked many years ago if she could follow your steps and learn enough to care for her children. But you, my wrinkle faced friend, said she was not strong enough. Not many years ago a young boy asked if he could walk with you for a while to learn of the plants that gave wellness medicines. Again you said no because you did not want to be bothered with a chatty child to feed while traveling the Good Medicine Road."

As he spoke these things to his reflection he realized how self-important he had felt and how ugly that kind of ego could be.

He looked away from the water and as he raised his eyes to the tree tops he began to remember others. He remembered a grandmother who came to sit at his feet while he tended those of her village. Always asking him what herb he was using and how he found it. He would answer the questions for a while, but then became so involved in the application of his medicine or his prayers or his ceremony, that he would say to her, "Woman, get me some of your hot stew and don't bother me until I finish my work."

As Wakhan Wichasa had this conversation with himself he realized he had been tricked by his own mind. Just as that tricky Magpie told stories no one could understand, his brain had kept him so busy he did not notice he had become self-centered. He thought only he could harvest correctly and offer wellness properly. He had no tolerance for the slow pace of women and children as he walked the valley or climbed the mountain. As he thought about those who had come forward asking to learn from him he was ashamed to realize he had turned them all away.

Wakhan Wichasa had forgotten that once he was young and curious and slow to understand. He forgot that others had taken time to share wisdom with him when he asked. He could remember how the elders were always patient and showed him many times how to know the plants in every season and how to harvest properly.

He mumbled to himself, as is common with folks who live alone, "You must live longer than you planned because you were foolish for too long." It was at that moment that Wakhan Wichasa realized he was anxious to give up his body and 'Cross the River' to be with Creator.

He puffed out a low groan as he rose on his stiff legs. He would simply have to get serious about this hunt for the right person and focus on the next generation and not on his own life. He gathered his many bundles and bags of medicine and tied them to the sash around his belly. It had sunk into his ribs and he realized his time was running out. His body was withering and he was becoming frail with age. That day he hiked over the mountain and down to the valley beyond his Looking Pool. When he arrived many children came running to call out his name and let the people of the village know he had arrived.

The Chief of this village was a young man called 'One with Many Horses'. He had taken his father's position of Chief after the elder 'Crossed the River' just the winter before. This young man had been interested in the Good Medicine Path for many years and was always full of questions when he was a child. When Wakhan Wichasa arrived at the lodge of the young chief he was greeted with warmth and smiles of welcome hospitality. As the chief gave him food and water they talked.

Wakhan Wichasa knew he must confess his arrogance and explain his need to share the Good Medicine before he left this world. Many Horses smiled as he watched the old man eating slowly with his few teeth and dropping food on his skinny chest as he spoke.

"You have taught many people the Good Medicine Ways my dear old friend! What silliness that you think you were arrogant," said Many Horses.

"Each one you tended had family or friends nearby as you gave those herbs and oils, roots and berries. While you dug in your medicine bags you talked away about where you found them and what they look like growing and how to harvest and prepare them for this kind of wellness. Some of the minerals that you fed us were from the ground-up stones of many colors and you always told us where they live," he continued.

Wakhan Wichasa was looking puzzled and stopped eating for a moment to think about this.

"I told people all these things?" He asked.

"Yes and much more, you always talk non-stop when you pray and when you offer wellness and when you are the ceremonies you have taught us. You do not like it when we ask too many questions and you do not like for us to travel with you, but you do not care if we follow at a distance and sparingly harvest what you have left behind. We remember how you said to never take the grandmother plant; only the young ones are for harvesting. You are not arrogant, you are simply preoccupied with your thoughts" said Many Horses.

"You have been a great teacher to many who have listened to your stories. There are healers in every village now and many who travel to gather the medicines you have shown us. We all respect you and honor the Good Medicine Way as you have taught us. There are some young women who have been following you for years. They walk quietly on the pathway behind you. They make no noise because they want to hear all your muttering words for they tell them how to harvest with respect for the next generation. They see how you always leave gifts for the plant nation and how you are grateful to Creator for every breath." Many Horses said.

Wakhan Wichasa's tummy was full and as he set his bowl aside, he gave a sigh of relief and thanked Creator for helping him to teach the next generation in this way. He wondered why he had never noticed that they were learning the medicine and how could he not know the young women were following him so close that they could hear his voice as he spoke to the Rooted Ones.

"I will return in the morning" said Wakhan Wichasa, "but tonight I must go to the big cedar tree by Looking Pond and become the ceremony of gratitude."

He rose on his thin and creaking legs to stand his full height and realized he was shorter than he remembered. Why was his mind so confused lately?

As he left the village children ran along singing his name and dancing in the dust. The noise they made covered that of the people who were following him into the forest. After he entered the cool shadows of the Standing Tall Ones he paused to listen for sounds of who might be following him. He heard only the sound of his own heartbeat and the breath of Creator that moved through him.

When he came to his camping spot he placed his medicine bags and bundles carefully on the grass and built a small fire. He wrapped his blanket close around his tired old bones and sat looking into the flames. He saw them dance with joy and sputter here and there with laughter. He knew the sound of fire so well and as he focused his mind he realized he was lost in fire's song. No wonder someone could be close by without him knowing, if all he listened to was fire. He focused his ears to the sounds around him but he was not hearing any Two Legged Ones.

That night Wakhan Wichasa asked Creator to protect

those who were following the Good Medicine Ways. As he slept he dreamed of the things he felt must be passed on. He would begin to invite the following ones to come to his fire so they could ask any questions that might help them with the medicine ways.

The next morning he heard that tribe of Magpies that always followed him and a laughing Crow. He wondered if they were laughing at his silly thoughts about his need for an apprentice. Wakhan Wichasa was beginning to forget to worry now. He was filled with gratitude for the ones who gathered the learning and for the way they had let him walk this Good Medicine Path as a Hollow Bone. Then he offered prayers of gratitude for the power of being a simple Hollow Bone. He thought of the gifts of the Hollow Bone and remembered the stories of how these gifts came to the Two Legged.

Ah Ho

That is only one way of saying the Hollow Bone legend. Wakhan Wichasa was living as a medicine man who believed he was a Hollow Bone. Following is the description story and belief of how a Hollow Bone serves as the vessel for Creator. It helps us understand what kind of people we should be. It is a way of guiding us to be in service to others. Those in the healing arts of Native tradition should endeavor to become a Hollow Bone.

"Gifts from the Hollow Bone"

The tribe had been blessed by a successful hunt that fall. Buffalo was offering her gifts to the people in many ways. Every member of the tribe knew how each piece of Buffalo should be used. Everyone shared in the work and everyone shared in the abundance of the rewards.

Many people had special talents and would direct one particular task. Maybe they were best at drying the meat, or making the hides into leather or preserving the organs. Whatever the task, each person would know they were working for the entire tribe. These lessons were taught to us by Ant. We learned to do our part to serve the whole by observing the cooperation of the Ant tribe.

On this fine day one of the Buffalo hides was stretched over poles to dry into a new rug to keep the Tipi of a young mother warm in the coming winter. Other hides were being stripped of their hair in preparation to become rawhide. The grandmothers were teaching the young mothers how to cut, clean and save this hair which would be used as padding for cradle boards, bedding and other things. Once the hair was removed this cleaned hide would be scraped and pounded on stones at the river for hours, where it would become clean, soft and flexible.

Working at the river was a social affair. Many prayers and songs were offered in gratitude to Buffalo. The children thought they were playing as they stomped in the water and run around falling, slipping, and sliding on the wet hide. Actually the game they played helped the mothers with the work of pounding the hide into softness. One of the hides would become a large drum. The children's laughter and the mother's smiles filled the hide with loving joy for the next generation and would resonate from the drum, in song.

When the hide was clean and soft many hands would work together to lift it out of the water and hang it across two raised logs, stretching it as best they could. Once the hide had cured (dried) it was solid and stiff like very thin and strong wood. The men were invited to participate in the next offering to this Buffalo hide. The women offered smudge to the men and thanked their hands for the hard work of hunting. Then they would smudge the raw hide that had spent four days hanging across the logs. Blessings were offered to everyone who handled this hide and to the Buffalo who wore it before it came to the people. This was an honorable way to prepare it for a sacred duty.

Now the men could take their sharp obsidian knives and cut two large circles from this hide. One circle would make the top (or head) of the large drum and one circle became the bottom. There would be much raw hide left after the circles were cut. Some of this raw hide could be cut into long strips to use as a binding to lace up the drum sides. Some of the strips could be saved to make into ropes or to tie the travois together for the next journey. None would be wasted. Once the circles were cut, holes were punched along the outer edge for lacing the drum together. Then the hide and lacings were taken back to the river for another soak. This soaking was to soften the hide so it would become pliable again and could be wrapped around the wooden hoop, which had been prepared earlier. After it was laced in place the drum would stand for four days to be blessed by Creator and to dry in preparation for its first song.

This large drum could be used for dances and ceremonies, prayers and offerings for the entire tribe. It would not sing with just one voice, it was to serve many. The Buffalo drum would be used for large tribal gatherings when several people would encircle it and in unison bring forward the rhythms of the tribe. The ancient songs of praise and honor to Creator would be lifted on the vibrations from Buffalo. The beat of the tribe's feet as they danced around the drum would help bring new heartbeats to the Buffalo tribe and bless Mother Earth. This gift of Buffalo had brought the heartbeat of Mother Earth to the people. She had given them a way to pray that would let Creator's ears be filled with joy.

The person who walks in a Hollow Bone Way carries these voices forward from the ancestors and is protected by their spirits. The gift of song, joy, dancing and praying will flow through the one who is a Hollow Bone. These gifts reach Mother Earth and 'All my Relations'. This is a natural process for the one who walks as a Hollow Bone.

Because more than one Buffalo was harvested during the hunt, there were several hides to attend to. Some of the hides would be tanned into heavy, yet soft leather. This leather was good for making the hammock that hung between the travois poles. These long, lodge pole, pines (or saplings) were laced together over the horse's neck so he could drag a heavy load. The gift of transportation and travel on the land represents the gift of spirit travel. This leather could be used for the sole of moccasins and would wear much longer than the softer deer hide used for the tops. The effort to make Buffalo leather was only expended when it was necessary. Many things could be done with the rawhide.

Those who live in the Hollow Bone Way bring the gift of spirit travel to everyone they meet. This spirit travel means we are walking the righteous path of Creator. It helps to remind us to give our soul the freedom to believe in Creator and to live in harmony with nature. We know we are participating in spirit travel when our daydreams and imagination bring us into the prayers of gratitude.

The gift of moving forward, not being stuck in old thinking or the past, are natural gifts that flow through the Hollow Bone. It takes no special effort or conscious thought for this to happen. Once the individual has heard this legend it automatically rests in the sub-conscious mind and is called forward when one simply thinks, 'Hollow Bone'.

To make Buffalo leather one first must offer ceremonies of gratitude and humbleness. Only then can they remove the brains from the skull. After the brain is removed, the skull will be placed on an ant hill where it will feed many little cousins. Once the skull is clean and bleached by Sun it will be honored in many ceremonies and used to dress Inipi (sweat lodge) altars.

Working with the brain shows the intelligence of Buffalo is being offered to the tribe. This is bringing forward our highest thoughts and intelligent thinking when we receive

Buffalo's gifts in the Hollow Bone Way. This allows us to think more clearly, make better choices and have positive thoughts. This means the tribe always knows where to find healthy food and water, where their tribe (community) is safest and how to rest without fear.

Buffalo is never lost for it has a perfect compass in its head. This helped the people always find their direction (physical and spiritual). Buffalo knows its child in a herd of several thousand. This reminds us that we are connected to the next generation. It reminds us that we are each unique to Creator and he will know our voice from all others.

Buffalo will circle the young ones if they are threatened by predators. They will stand with heads down, horns forward, facing out, to protect the young ones from harm and this will preserve the next generation. This is a reminder to provide for and protect those who are smaller, younger, and less fortunate than us. It also reminds us that Creator is caring for all our needs as well as protecting Mother Earth for the next generation.

Buffalo is able to smell sweet-grass or water or even dusting baths, for hundreds of miles and will walk in single-minded tribal fashion for days to reach the goal. This example of Buffalo Medicine gives us stamina and helps us reach the goals of life. This gift tells us to walk with those who are in harmony with us. Many gifts of intelligence came to the people when they honored Buffalo by dressing the skull and using the brains for tanning. Anytime we are aware of our body as the Hollow Bone we are filtering out the foolish thinking of anger or resentment and focusing on gratitude and love.

Ant brought many gifts to the people because he was the worker who cleaned the skull. Now the people knew how to work together for the good of the tribe. They understood about protecting the unborn and the importance of the young warriors bringing food to the elders and children. The teachings of ant give us the gifts of co-operation, team work, balanced relationships, and attention to detail. The combined lessons from Ant and Buffalo come to the one who is mindful that they are the Hollow Bone.

The brains (protein and enzymes) from the skull mixed with ash (lye) from the campfire and added to water would make a paste. This paste would be spread on the inside of the well-scraped rawhide. Then they fold the hide, with paste side in, and soak it in strong salt brine for a couple weeks. Then the hide is taken back to the fresh water river and rinsed many times. Then, the hide is placed over a log and burnish with smooth sticks until it is nearly dry. This is how the hide becomes soft leather.

Some salt brine pools were natural on the landscape near hot springs. Others could be made by salting a small pool of water. This was done only when other adequate drinking water was nearby. Unfortunately the white man would later think the Indian people had purposely poisoned water supplies. These salted pools could soak a hide for the required time to break down the tissue and allow it to become thick, soft, and pliable leather. Many rains and one winter would re-sweeten the water, so this temporary working pool was not spoiled permanently. This helped the people understand that everything is in a cycle with Mother Earth and that we can use what she offers as long as we understand it can be regenerated. They would never kill the last fresh water pool in an area. The Hollow Bone person is offering a subtle ecological lesson to themselves and the world.

The hooves of Buffalo could be boiled with pitch from trees and made into glue, or dried to be filled with pebbles and covered with leather for a child's rattle. Horns could be carved into spoons and dippers. Ears could be sewn shut on one end, whip-stitched partially closed on the other and dried over a tree limb to make fur lined moccasins for small feet in winter (up to about women's size 5). The tail was a good quirt for horsemen and the scrotum was made into a man's carry bag for sacred herbs. These least likely parts of Buffalo were sometimes the greatest gifts. Reminding the people that no one and nothing is worthless. Each has something special to offer. All of these gifts had come from the outside of Buffalo. When the Hollow Bone healer is offering wellness to the physical body, they bring all of these gifts to the individual on an energetic level.

The first gifts from the inside of Buffalo were gathered by the elders who served as medicine men and women. The elders had chosen various organs to make into medicine, each with its own use. The heart would be gifted to the hunter who had killed the Buffalo. This would help them remember they were related to Buffalo, because now the heart of Buffalo lived in the hunter.

The heart of any animal does not need to be 'aged' or cured before it is eaten. It can be eaten the same day as the kill. Other meat (even modern day beef) must be allowed to slowly cool and rest for a few days (cure) prior to butchering to kill certain microbes that can cause illness in humans. Seven days for wild game, and three days for domestic animals is the general rule. This is because of the adrenaline and other hormones and enzymes as well as living parasites and microbes that are diffused throughout the muscle (meat) prior to death. It will cause illness in those who eat it, such as diarrhea. Because the blood was pumping quickly through the heart (running prior to death is normal in most wild game) the hormones were dispersed to the muscle tissue and not accumulated in the heart.

Some of the liver could be eaten fresh, just as the heart, but the abundance of a good hunt would allow some liver to be preserved. It would be smoked and dried over the fire and then ground into a fine powder. This powder could later be made into a broth to serve as a tonic for someone with weakness or thin blood (possibly anemia).

The gall bladder was done the same way to serve those with swollen or painful joints (possibly gout, arthritis, or rheumatism). Kidneys would be eaten fresh or dried for later use in a mixture called pemmican (high source of protein).

Each organ has a use and the medicine people of the tribe understood how to harvest and preserve it for the wellness of the tribe. This reminded the people that when one responsibility is complete (the organ serving life to Buffalo) that they can always find a way to be of more use. The medicines of Buffalo that heal illness and injury help support a healthy immune system. It was even a way to understand how the human body worked as they carefully dissected the various animals that had been killed for food.

Buffalo is so generous she has two stomach pouches (actually four chambered ruminant system) for the people to make into water containers. Once washed and cleaned these pouches could be filled with sand and left in the sun to dry and harden. This thick rawhide pouch can then be sealed with pitch or resin on the outside to create a water proof surface. A sand stone would be rubbed on the inside of the pouch until it was smooth as glass. Then sinew made from tendons (strong thread-like material) would be whip-stitched around the upper edge to protect the vessel from ripping at the edges. Some pouches were left raw (not covered with pitch) and could be carried like a bag when filled with water. These raw stomach pouches would dry flat for easy storage and yet, in only moments, they would re-soften when dipped in water.

The people understood the importance of not camping right on the water source. This was a way to protect the water from pollution by the tribe. It would be easier to camp close to the water and simply dip it out as needed, rather than camping several hundred yards away and hand carrying water over the distance. But always being willing to do the extra work required to protect Mother Earth was an honorable way to live. Buffalo tried to make this work easier for the people. A person living in the Hollow Bone way offers this respect for Mother Earth at every opportunity. They have no fear of working hard and they are willing to care for the pure water.

As the men helped the women cut meat from the bone, women began making a hardy Buffalo stew from the organs that were not needed by the medicine people. Some of the meat would be cut into strips and dried over smoking fires with salt and dried herbs (spices) added for flavor. This method of preserving the meat made it light and easy to carry for the nomadic plains tribes. It would be similar to our modern day jerky. This method also preserved it for winter when hunting would be difficult. Understanding how to plan ahead and preserve the gifts of 'now' is an important lesson for those who walk the Hollow Bone way. Giving us the ability to plan ahead helps offer us security for survival.

Once the meat for the cooking pot is removed from the bones, the bones are given to the dogs or left outside the camp circle for Coyote and Wolf. After the bones have been chewed by the animals and all the scraps are gleaned, they chew off both ends of the bone as they try to get to the rich marrow center. Some of the bones would have been boiled by the tribe to collect this fat-enriched substance for use in a healing poultice, for grease used in cooking and for the 'medicine' offered to ill children (high vitamin/mineral content, tonic). There might be more meat left on the bones than the canines could eat at one meal so they would bury the bone. Then all the little Creepy Crawly Tribe (a Native term for insects) eats the remaining tissue. This gift is a reminder that we have all the abundance for today and for the future, so we can generously offer our abundance to others. It helps us to be generous and hospitable.

Finally the winter freeze arrives and purifies the bone in its buried hole inside Mother Earth. Freezing kills all the germs and anything that could cause illness or harm. This reminder is about the temperature of winter. Coldness of winter kills germs and therefore we understand how the cold water or snow packs, or cold stones pressed into an injury can kill pain, remove swelling and inflammation. We are reminded to hibernate and rest in the winter so we can be reborn in the next season.

At last the rains of spring wash over the resting place of the buried bone, washing away the dirt. In the spring season, the bone surfaces as a solid calcium tube of hollowness. Before long, summer sun takes over and bleaches it pure white. Finally, the fall winds blow across it and the four seasons have cleaned, blessed, and created the Hollow Bone.

This Hollow Bone has nothing in its center to hinder the flow of Creator's voice (the wind). It is open at both ends and now encases only energy as it passes through. It has no energy of its own now, so it is available for Creator to enhance. The bone has passed through all four seasons in preparation for its new service as a teacher. It teaches us that we are not the healing power, which comes from the Source; we are simply the "Hollow Bone" allowing the Source to move through us. This humbleness is passed on to Mother Earth and all her inhabitants when an individual lives as a Hollow Bone.

In the fall, young hunters collect the dried bones from the surface of Mother Earth. They might seem to be worthless at this point. There is no food value as even the Creepy Crawlies have left, and Coyote is not interested. This empty Hollow Bone looks pretty and pure and white, but it has no value. Yet the young men will gather them in fall to work with during the long quiet winter months. It is only in this condition that the young hunters can bring the bones to camp and make them into the tools needed to serve the people. The bone can be broken with stone clubs and then the pieces shaped by scraping them on rough flat stones. In this way the bones are made into sewing needles, scraping knives, leather punches, and even beads for decorations.

It was only after the bone became worthless, hollow, open, and empty that it could be made into a tool. This is how some Native people see themselves. The people try to clear and clean the spirit and heart of all greed, ego, arrogance, selfishness, self-pity, hate, or anger so they can become a tool for Creator. Creator can breathe His breath of love, compassion, generosity, hospitality, and honor into the Hollow Bone. This kind of tool can serve wellness to others for it is in perfect balance.

All of these gifts are offered to us from the ancestors and from Buffalo, through a single thought by the One Who Walks in the Hollow Bone Way. The one who is seeking to be a Hollow Bone can simply take in a deep breath and allow the air to flow out as it purifies the Hollow Bone of their human body. They will fill their heart with the desire to serve and they will be safely protected from any harm. All of the gifts from Buffalo and the Hollow Bone will reach into Mother Earth on that one breath.

Buffalo offers physical, spiritual, and emotional food for our balanced life. When you live in the tradition of the Hollow Bone, you invite all the gifts of Buffalo to go into every living thing. These gifts first flow through your body. This is one way Native People stay in balance and feel protected while they serve others.

It is as if the human body is protected by Buffalo's thick hide. The human body is glued back together or re-connected with Creator and Mother Earth through prayer and dance and the glue made of Buffalo hooves. These are the 'outside' gifts from Buffalo's body. The body is fed with the meat, healed with special medicines from the organs, brought tools for drinking water (the stomach bags, horn dippers, and spoons) and reminded to be a Hollow Bone; all from the 'inside' gifts from Buffalo. The medicines of strength, endurance, power, and intelligence from Buffalo, gained through using the brain, come to the one walking in the Hollow Bone Way.

The gifts of following the seasons as the bone was buried by dog or wolf and then found resting on Mother Earth are brought in to help balance the body and spirit with nature. The Medicine Wheel and the altar are holding space for you as the offerings of prayer are made because you are following the ancestor's teachings. The skull on every Inipi (Sweat Lodge) altar will send blessings to the world. The vibrations of your breath can touch even those you do not see.

Here are a few exercises to open the way of the Hollow Bone to you. Sit quietly with your eyes closed and take a little journey through your imagination. Envision your whole being as a strong Hollow Bone. See the pure white, sun bleached power of your solid body. Notice how all thoughts of guilt, and shame, or negative thinking can flow through you and out your feet, down into Mother Earth where they disappear as her food. You are empty of any improper thinking and filled only with the voice, breath, and blessings of Creator. You are safe from any outside force.

It is wonderful if you can stay mindful of this image if you are in service work or healing work. It is here in this consciousness that you will occasionally be able to actually witness a healing experience for your client. It is here in the Hollow Bone image of yourself that you will remain 'you' and not confuse your client's burdens with your own. It is impossible for you to pick up your clients symptoms or illnesses if you are safely detached as the Hollow Bone. The energy only flows one way, from Creator above, down through the Hollow Bone and out your hands to the client and through them down into Mother Earth. This is a learned skill and so it is easy for you to participate in the Hollow Bone Way. The practice necessary to become a Hollow Bone can empower any practitioner who wishes to live a healthy life while serving those who are ill or injured.

Some practice sessions you can do to strengthen your awareness of being a Hollow Bone are helpful. One used by young children and new students is to sit quietly in nature where you can hear animal sounds. Generally even a park in the city will have a few chattering birds or squirrels. If it is not possible for you to go out in nature, then buy a CD of nature sounds.

Find a comfortable place to sit or recline where you will not be disturbed. Close your eyes, and take two or three deep slow breaths through your nose, releasing them out your mouth. Imagine your body as a Hollow Bone. As you sit quietly take an inventory of your body and let each ache or pain or discomfort float down the Hollow Bone into Mother Earth. Let your being become empty of agenda, worry, sadness, and stress. It is great if you know the difference in the song of Robin and Blue Jay, but you do not need to know them by name. Just note 'bird', 'squirrel', 'monkey', or whoever lives in your area or has been recorded on the CD.

Then as they become the sounds filling your ears let the vibration of these voices fill your heart. Let them clear and clean the Hollow Bone as the ant did for Buffalo skull. Let them take every bit of darkness away. Not one grain of sand is sticking to the inside of this perfect, empty, clean, Hollow Bone. With eyes closed and breathing deeply you will let the sound flow through you. Imagine how pure and clear you are. It is important to focus on relaxing the muscles of your mouth and tongue, as if you have no words to speak, only the freedom of letting go.

Within a few sessions you will notice that your personal thinking is gone and you are feeling the vibrations of the animals and are focused totally on the sounds they are making. There is no room in the Hollow Bone for old thinking of laziness, self-pity, addiction, denial, anger or any other negative thought. There is no space for judgment, fear, or even love if it is filled with the animal vibrations.

You only experience the neutral flow of sound and vibration as energy. You are not making the sound move through you but rather are allowing the sound to flow through you. This is a very relaxing exercise and can be quite enlightening. Remember it is not forced meditation or even prayer. You are simply allowing natural sounds to flow through the Hollow Bone. This encourages the mind to be still and helps you feel the energy of vibrations moving through your body. If you find your mind trying to make words or chatter, just look at the image of the Hollow Bone in your mind and think how clean, hollow, pure, white, and silently empty it is. These are words with no agenda; they are helping to blank out the thinking processes. In our modern society it is important to find space to simply be and not have to deal with the anxiety of thought.

After you have done this exercise a few times, you will be able to have an instant version of it any time that you wish to relax. (You can use Native drum and flute music for this same exercise if you wish.)

Another method to exercise your Hollow Bone muscle is to practice letting go of thoughts. As you are working or driving, relaxing, or trying to go to sleep at night, you hear conversation in your mind about the test you need to take next week, the work load on your desk or the grocery shopping you must do after work. Just take a deep breath and let it blow out the 'words' that are making noise in your head. Let the feeling of air moving through your whole body be the focus of your energy.

Do not argue with the 'brain', just acknowledge it and let the 'mind' bring you closer to Spirit with your breath. You can make the brain 'mind' if you discipline it regularly. As you breathe out language, breathe in 'emptiness'. Think of the Hollow Bone and how you are a conduit for Creator. This is very effective for bringing you back to focus on your spirit from a non-judgmental space and can help relax your body as well. It is easy to see words in the form of letters falling out the bottom of the Hollow Bone and melting into Mother Earth like snowflakes on warmed soil. Enjoy the freshness of the breath that is sweeping in from above and through the Hollow Bone. Use your imagination to envision yourself as the pure, white Hollow Bone.

This energy that Native people say is 'Creator's

breath' has many names. In some cultures it is called Ki, Chi, Paraná, or life force. In the Native way it is considered Wakhan (Sacred). The fact that so many indigenous cultures knew that the flow of energy moving through the body could be directed to support wellness in themselves and others, indicates that it exists. Science describes this as our neurological system and recognizes the electricity that flows through each body. The Native Way of envisioning the Hollow Bone and consciously allowing energy to move through the body is relaxing and balancing for body, mind, and spirit. This is a way to maintain healthy boundaries and not become entangled in other people's expectations or resentments. It is a way to be detached from society's negative influences.

This may sound like a contradiction. How can you be compassionate and alert to others needs if you are detached? Think about this, the mother cannot comfort and heal her child with an injury if she is feeling the same pain. She must keep her wits about her to think of how to best alleviate the pain while still loving the child. Just like putting on your oxygen mask first, before helping others on the airplane, you must be safe before you can offer safety to others. It is this conscious effort to serve the injured without participation in the injury that makes one a 'healer' in the Hollow Bone Way.

Selfish Chief

The first time I heard this story was at a Pow-Wow gathering in Wallowa, Oregon. Tazz had shared a funny story and everyone was laughing and bragging about how good Indians were. A woman spoke up and said she knew one that shows how human we really are. She said you should never get a big head about being Indian.

I never knew this elders name but she was from Mission, Oregon out on the Umatilla reservation. Since that is a confederate tribe she could have been from several different tribes. I do not know for sure who to give credit for this legend.

I always liked this legend. I love the humor and the lessons and the quick wit at the end. But my dad did not care for this story. He said it was not really typical of the animal stories he knew and he would never tell it and would cringe when I did.

Once there was a Chief called Selfish who thought his family was better than all the rest of the tribe. He demanded the best of everything be kept for him and his family. He forgot that he was the one chosen to serve his tribe. He forgot he was supposed to always think of others first. A leader must always give to those he leads or they will not follow for long. Someone had to teach this lesson to old chief Selfish.

Selfish made all the hunters bring their prizes to his lodge where he took the first choice of all the meat. He would keep more than his share of the health-giving fat and his body was growing larger and larger because of it.

Selfish did not think he was fat and he pretended to be humble, as he would bless each hunter when they came to his tipi. Selfish had a wife. This one, who should be honored to be the wife of a Chief, was actually not honorable at all. When she went gathering with the others, she would sit in the shade and call the younger ones to her. "Bring your basket so I can take the best share for my husband, your Chief. It is your duty to honor him with these gifts." She would puff out her fat lip mouth as she spoke.

Then she would sit and eat as many berries or roots as she could stuff in her fat face before she would fill the basket for the Chief.

When a Chief who loves his tribe and lives in honor and respect and is leading a tribe, they love him and his family very much. They try to give him the best of everything. A good and loving Chief would never need to ask for anything, as all the tribe would watch for ways to serve him in return for his care of the People.

When one is greedy and thinks he is better than anyone else, he is asking Creator to teach him with humiliation. Being humble is much easier than being humiliated. This Chief had much to learn. When some moons had passed, his daughter grew up. She was very beautiful and many wanted to marry her. Some of them were selfish too, because they were learning this bad habit from the example set by their Chief. They guessed if they married the daughter of Selfish, they could be rich and spoiled, too.

The Princess (a Chief's daughter is known as a

princess) of the tribe was not selfish and greedy like her parents. She was ashamed of their ways and tried to be very giving and generous when her parents were not watching. The daughter was called Princess Jay and she loved one called Blue Jay. She knew her father would never let her marry Blue Jay.

He was from a neighboring tribe and if they married, Blue Jay would be living with Selfish and his tribe. The old traditions taught that it was harder for a mother to lose a daughter than a son. So when a couple was married, they went to live with the mother of the wife.

The neighboring tribe, family of Blue Jay, had told many stories about old Selfish and his misdeeds. None of the tribes would trade with him because he treated them so poorly. Princess Jay's father wanted her to marry one of the boys he had chosen for her. This way, he could keep his selfish ways. He would not be influenced by any outsider who might see through his fake humbleness and know he was selfish.

Princess Jay came up with a plan and one day told her love about it in quiet whispers. Then she went to her father and asked, "Have you chosen my mate yet father?"

"No daughter" he said. "Are you in such a hurry to leave your fathers lodge?" he asked.

"Oh no father, it is the best lodge in the community and is stocked better than any three other lodges together," she humbly answered while giving him the flattery he desired.

"Then what is your question about daughter?" he asked.

She answered, "You should have a grandson to play with during your old age, my father, and a son to take over your hard work when you are tired. You have provided for all my needs, father. Now, I think you should choose a husband for me who can help provide for your needs."

"A-Ay" he said with a big smile. This sounded like

more people to pamper him and to make him even richer.

"I have been dreaming of a wonderful way for the choice to be made," said Princess Jay. "We could have a big feast with all the tribes. They could all bring an abundance of food. We could dance and drum and sing songs with the flute players," she said, knowing her father loved these gatherings when he could eat himself to exhaustion.

"Ay go on daughter, tell me more. This may be a good thing you have dreamed," he said sitting up slightly from his resting place, to better see her beautiful face.

"I thought if we held a contest with all the men from all the tribes who would wish to marry me, you could see who is the most deserving," she said, again flattering his giant ego.

He puffed out his cheeks with pride in this wise daughter but did not speak.

She continued, "We could have a race and the one who is fastest would win me as his bride. I know how you need a strong and wise man to marry me, so when the time comes for you to make your final journey 'Across the River', you can be proud of whom you have chosen to take care of me and your grandchildren."

When Princess Jay spoke of his final journey 'Across the River' she was speaking of his death. For Indian people believe that their ancestors have crossed a great river to stand with Creator for all of eternity, where they look after the future generations.

"I have raised a wise daughter," said the selfish old chief. "Go and make all the arrangements and tell all the young men they need to participate. I want the best man in our tribe to be my son-in-law" he smiled while in his mind, he began to plan and scheme.

"Ay but father, let's invite those of every tribe. Some of the others have foods we do not have. Some live in berry country and others in seed lands" she said. "Some might bring gifts of Sage, Tobacco, or even Turquoise".

"You could hold the grandest of all celebrations and have each one who wishes to marry me compete in this race to win me. We would tell them that all who want to race have to present themselves to you with a gift before they are allowed to run. They could bring you many gifts!" she said shyly looking at the floor of the lodge. She did not want her father to see her eyes telling the truth behind her plan.

"Not only are you wise about how to fairly choose a mate, but also in thinking of security for your family!" he smiled. "What a good daughter you are. Go make this feast as large as you wish, and invite those of all tribes near and far. You will have the best man in the whole world if he comes to your feast," he said. All the while thinking of the greedy boy named Bear that he had in mind for his daughter.

She replied, "Ah ho father, he will come." She ran out the door of the lodge and all the way to the river where, hidden in a tree, she found her love, Blue Jay.

Blue Jay and Princess Jay talked about how he could win because she would set out a hard course for all the contestants and only he would know the short cut. She would require all of the racers to bring something from each area of the land, to prove he had been there.

They planned how Blue Jay would be sure to win. They decided what gifts she should ask for and where they should come from. Then, after her sweet Blue Jay had gathered all these things in abundance and hidden them near the finish line, she would call for the time of feasting.

She had learned these scheming ways from her father and knew her father would be planning his own scheme. She knew of his plan to marry her off to that silly old Bear who was lazy all winter and always eating the sweet honey so he was fat like her father.

Princess Jay was not disappointed. She heard her selfish father talking one night outside her tipi when he thought she was sleeping. "You can hide near the finish line and when you see the one who would win just cut in front of him and you will come in first" said that old Selfish Chief.

Princess Jay knew he must be talking to the one named Bear because he was grunting away as her father spoke. He was a bully, always pushing his way to the front of the lines of fishermen on the banks of the river so he could get the finest salmon. Bear was not a good choice for her, but he was always making gifts to her selfish father so she knew he was the one who her father would choose.

When the time was right, all the young men were invited and they came from nearby and far away to seek this wealthy princess as a mate. Many dancers and drummers had come to give voice and join in the event. Many songs of bravery and strength were sung. Stories of other young brides who made wise choices were told, and stories of some not-so-wise made much laughter fill the air.

On the second day of the gathering, Selfish called for everyone's attention.

"I want you all to listen to my daughter," He yelled out. "She is the daughter of the richest Chief and she is the most beautiful in all the Nations. She is very wise and I am proud of her. She has decided that I should choose the best man in this world for her. So this man will be chosen only after he proves himself worthy. I will have her tell you the rules of this game. The winner will be as my son. He will be mate of my daughter, son of my wife, father of my grandchildren and one day, Chief of this tribe" he called out in his fat, huffy, puffy voice.

Princess Jay stepped forward and the gathering gasped at her beauty. She had such a brilliant blue-black set of feathers adorning her head that she seemed to glow. Down to the tips of her toes were soft delicate feathers, each carefully laid one on top of the other. Her black eyes sparkled with excitement as she told the contestants what she wanted.

"I want the most sacred piece of Pipe Stone from the mountain where it grows and the most beautiful Crystal from Healing Waters River. I want these Stone People wrapped in the longest Sweet Grass braids from Sweet Grass Meadow for my wedding gift," she said timidly looking down at the ground but peeking out the corner of her eyes at Blue Jay.

"Ay, listen to my child as she is not greedy. She is only wise to want the best. I will be the one to judge who brings the best gifts. But the only one allowed to present me with the best gift is the winner of this race" he puffed between his fat lips. Selfish Chief knew he had the best of all these things and would provide them to the selfish boy called Bear. Old Selfish Chief would help Bear trick the others and win the race.

"I am looking for the very bravest and wisest and strongest man to be my mate," she said. "But these gifts will be offered to my people as a promise that the new chief will always think of sacred things and be willing to share with all his people."

Selfish thought his daughter was just trying to impress the people. He was not interested in her silly words and motioned for Bear to come to his side.

Bear came running forward and stood tall while pounding his chest, "Look at my mighty strength. No one can beat me. I will run your race and not get tired because of my powerful legs," he yelled. He was standing so close to Princess Jay that she could smell his fishy breath.

All the guests clapped and cheered at his confidence. With that, the one called Wolf ran to the front saying, "I may not look as strong as the others, but I can run fast for a very long time. I will be the one to call the beautiful Princess Jay my mate for my legs hold endurance" and he bowed his head to her as he stepped back.

She looked up shocked to see Blue Jay step forward. She did not like all this boasting and wished he would have been quiet. But as soon as he came to the front, she was impressed. He wore an outfit that reflected her beauty.

Many stood back in awe as they saw him come forward also dressed head to toe in shiny blue-black feathers.

They looked as if they were already mates. He had placed black moss over his legs, under his fine feather outfit, and they looked to be the strongest legs of all the competitors.

She felt a surge of love and looked to the ground to hide a blush.

"I come to say that I will serve this good woman and her tribe all the days of my life if I should win this race" he stated.

With that, Selfish said "Enough of this bragging! Daughter, tell them what they must do to claim you as their mate". He thought she would draw lines in the dirt and the one who ran fastest would be the winner. He knew if the crowds were close to the edges that Bear could pop in at the last second and win the race. He planned to make a distracting war hoop to give Bear a chance to take the lead.

"Ay" said Princess Jay "You honor me by coming to this game; to ask for me as your mate. All who have come forward with gifts for my father to request a place in this race are brave men and all shall be honored with a fine feast and much dancing when you return. We will make stories and legends about each one of you to tell the children. I am only sorry that I can have but one mate!" and everyone laughed with her.

Her voice sparkled as she spoke and all the young men and some of the elders were in love with Princess Jay at that very moment.

"You will each run to the top of Pipe Stone Mountain and collect your piece of sacred Pipe Stone. This Pipe Stone will be used to make a sacred pipe for this tribe so we might always remember our ancestors," she said with great reverence.

Princess Jay did not hear her father gasp as he saw a dent in his scheme. He had the best piece of Pipe Stone but he did not want it carved as a pipe for the tribe. He wanted a beautiful image made just for himself.

"Then you must each run to Healing Waters River in

the valley below and find the purest, most clear crystal stone. With this stone I can tend our tribes' wounds and help us all stay well," called out Princess Jay.

The crowd cheered at her wisdom and laughed at the difficult task she was preparing for the young men who had come to claim her as a mate.

Now Selfish was getting edgy. "How could she have thought to make these young men run such a difficult race?" He wondered silently. He knew there was not a larger or more perfect Crystal in all the Stone Tribe than one he had managed to take from Bear. But he wanted it for his own healing not the healing of others.

Then Princess Jay said, "You will want to rest and drink from the river, for your next task is to hike over to Sweet Grass Meadow and bring me three long braids. These braids will remind us of the unity in our tribe and of the sacred herbs on our Mother Earth that feed us all. While you sit and braid this sacred sweet-grass, think of the shortest way back to this place to prove how wise you are by being the first one to arrive with all these gifts. The one who brings the best gifts across the line first and still has the strength to carry me across the river on his back will have me as his mate. Rest tonight and sing your prayers, for the race will start in the morning".

Selfish had stumbled back to sit on top of his giant pile of furs and pelts. All the furs and pelts were gifts from the young men who came to seek his daughter's pleasure. What was this daughter doing to his plan? He could say nothing to stop the race now or he would be humiliated. He would need to give the gifts of his best pipe stone, favorite crystal, and longest sweet grass braids to Bear before he left on this race. He hoped that Bear was smart enough to find a safe place to hide until the runners were near the finish line. He gave a quick sign to Bear so he would come behind the Chiefs lodge for a talk. When Bear came around the corner with his silly grinning face, Selfish began to worry a bit.

"Here, take these gifts to bring back to my daughter" He said as he pushed his best treasures into Bears giant hands.

"Then go find a place close to the finish line to hide until I give you a war hoop. When you hear my voice, jump in the race and cross the finish line first," he whispered to Bear.

"I can go straight to Sweet Grass Meadow and wait for the tired runners there and win the race fine from that point," said Bear with his own selfish pride beginning to show.

"No, don't risk getting beaten. Go a little way down the trail with the others and then ...." His voice trailed off as he saw that rude Blue Jay from the neighboring tribe walking close.

"I will be fine and do just as you say my Chief," said Bear as he lumbered his way back into the crowd. Bear would not let Selfish push him around. He would rest tonight and then go to Sweet Grass Meadow to make it appear he had run the entire race.

A great cheer went up from the gathering the next morning as the racers took their places. All the People from all the tribes were filled with excitement. Many of the men had already hit the trail before the crowd could even say best wishes to them.

The gathering began to prepare for the return of the young men. They were betting among themselves on who would win and who they hoped would win.

Many of the women were saying how they wished the one called Blue Jay would win. He was so beautiful standing next to Princess Jay and they thought him to be a smart and talented man. He could lead the tribe with much more joy than Selfish ever had.

Time went by slowly for Princess Jay as she watched the horizon for the first sign of the winner. She knew it would be Blue Jay for they had made great plans. He had gathered the Stone People from all the places on her race track.

He had searched for the finest, most amazing Crystal from Healing Waters River. He was sure it had powers that his beautiful Princess Jay could use to keep wellness alive for her people. When he harvested the sacred Pipe Stone, he wept because of the power he saw revealed in its beauty. He would be the one to carve this stone into the most sacred pipe, as his personal gift to the people of his mate.

Because he had spent days seeking the most glorious gifts, he had confidence that they would be seen as the best. On race day, he could go directly to Sweet Grass Meadow and begin the braids as the final gift. He did not want to get back too soon or he might be accused of cheating. Because he had ran off first up the trail, some thought he would win. He was smart enough to get a good head start while the others stood around taking bows to the cheering crowd and showing off their muscled legs!

Blue Jay had gone the day before and left one of his shiny blue feathers in plain sight at each location where the runners were sure to see it. When one would arrive and see Blue Jay's feather, he would announce to the others that Blue Jay was up ahead and they better hurry. This was, of course, the plan so Blue Jay was not suspected of cheating.

Bear had not been seen by any of the runners from the moment they left the village. Bear had gone straight to Sweet Grass Meadow, but he had taken his time and stopped to inspect several ant hills to see if they had laid their eggs yet. By the time he got to Sweet Grass Meadow, Blue Jay was already there making long beautiful fresh sweet grass braids. He decided to hide out for a few minutes so other runners could see him as he pretended to run to the meadow.

When the first of the runners topped the hill of Sweet Grass Meadow and found Blue Jay finishing his Sweet Grass braids, they knew who the winner was to be.

Blue Jay was pretending to huff and puff, as if he had

been racing at top speed. When he stood to leave and waved back at the other runners, he took one last peak in his pouch for the stones. He felt deep down and then looked on the ground where he had been sitting. They were not there. How could this be? What had happened to his perfect plan? What would happen to his lovely Princess Jay? If he returned without the stones, he could not claim her as his mate. How could he have been so over confident as to have forgotten the stones? He knew he had left them in the tree where he met his lovely Princess Jay the night before the race. His love for her had made him forget his treasures. Now what would he do?

He made his heart calm down and his shaking breath be still. He thought for a moment on how he could use his good mind to overcome this problem. He realized he could still give these fine Stone People to Princess Jay after they were married. But for now, he would need to use his best efforts to come up with a new plan. He was not used to tricks and schemes. So he tried to think of what his friend Coyote would do. It came to him that he would need to wait for more of the racers to arrive before he could try his plan.

It was a risk because the fastest would arrive first. But they had been running all day while he rested in Sweet Grass Meadow, so he was confident he could speak to them and, if his plan worked, he would still be able to win over his tired competitors. While he waited for more to arrive, he helped his cousins gather long blades of grass for their braids.

"Go ahead Blue Jay! You were leading the race ahead of us all day. We have found your dropped feathers along the trail where you went so fast that they fell from your outfit. We all know you can win the Princess. You do not need to take your time to help us," They said.

Blue Jay was feeling guilty for the trick he was about to play on his cousins, but he could not let Princess Jay become another man's wife. If he came back without the gifts of the best Pipe Stone, Crystal and Sweet Grass, he could not win the race even if he did cross the finish line first.

When many runners had arrived but no one was finished braiding their Sweet Grass, he called to them. "My brothers and cousins, come here so we can talk. That Selfish old Chief may not be honorable with us at the end of our race."

There was a lot of mumbling and cursing among the young ones for they knew Blue Jay was right. They must find a plan to make sure that Selfish would follow through on his promise and give his daughter in marriage.

"If you think you are the smartest one" said clumsy Bear as he lay on his back huffing and puffing from his very short run, "You tell us a plan and we will go along with it to make this Chief give up his daughter." Bear had no intention of going along with any plan but now he was worried because he had waited too long and all the runners were arriving in Sweet Grass Meadow.

Blue Jay pretended to be thinking when he suddenly perked up and said, "I have it! Let us put all our gatherings in a circle and we will choose among them to make four perfect sets. We will choose the four most sacred pieces of Pipe Stone and the four best healing Crystal Stones. Then we will choose the longest Sweet Grass Braids. Each one of us will have a set, but we will be witness that these four sets are the most perfect. That way Selfish cannot find fault with any of the gathering gifts and he will not be able to take back our reward."

"That is a good plan to keep him honest but how will we know who gets one of the four perfect sets?" asked Frog Boy who had just arrived.

"It seems fair that since Blue Jay has been in the lead and he is the one with the idea that he should be one of the four" said Owl Man.

"Ay" said everyone.

"And the three sets that are left will be won in a stick

game. Blue Jay will need to wait until the game is over so we know who is racing with him. This will give us all time to rest as well and come in not looking so badly beaten," said Owl Man.

Soon everyone was emptying their pouches into the circle and Blue Jay pretended to do the same. When the four perfect sets were chosen, the other items that had been gathered were left on the ground for everyone knew they did not have a chance to win. Some just left their hard-won treasure on Mother Earth, hoping for a blessing. They all knew that their unity would help serve to keep old Selfish honest. It was more important to replace Selfish as Chief of the tribe than it was to be the one chosen to marry his daughter.

With the best of the best in his medicine pouch for safe keeping, Blue Jay felt a bit of guilt over his trickery. But the stick games were fun to watch and being a joyful fellow, he soon was cheering on the finalists in the stick game. Before long, he had his last three competitors.

Clumsy old Bear had won and even though he had no chance to win the last leg of the race, he was determined to try. No one begrudged him this honor, as he was an easy fellow even if he was a bit too friendly with Selfish. The next perfect set of sacred items went to Owl Man.

This put the first frown on Blue Jays face. He knew that Owl Man was even wiser than he and that he was honest as well but could definitely pull off a trick if need be. He would need to be very careful in his dance to glory or he could still lose his lovely Princess Jay.

Everyone was surprised when young Frog Boy won the fourth and final set of perfect gifts. They all felt he was too young to marry and they did not think he had enough energy to even finish the race. Blue Jay stepped up to defend the boy who was not quite a man.

"Listen, my brothers! No one said the Princess would marry her choice this day. He may have time to grow up before that day arrives and he did win the stick game fairly," he sang out with a bit of laughter.

Everyone joined in the laughter and Blue Jay was confident he could win over this man boy, so all was going well.

When all was finished, the winners of the four perfect bundles lined up to start the race. They looked at each other and made jokes, "Good luck my brothers, but not as good as my luck" called Blue Jay as he fairly flew down the trail.

"Have a fast run but not as fast as mine," yelled Bear as he began a full out run for the trail.

"Have a good race but not as good as mine" called Frog Boy as he hopped on the trail.

"Be wise at each turn but not as wise as me" cried Owl Man as he silently flew by.

They were fairly close for a long way but as they entered the forest, Bear was slowing down and had begun to crash through the underbrush. This was causing Owl Man and Blue Jay to separate a bit so they could navigate more cautiously.

Blue Jay was glad for the separation as it meant he could get to the short-cut and be at the finish line without Frog Boy or Owl Man seeing the way.

Blue Jay was glad he was fresh from resting all day and soon he had started on the short-cut path. He had only rounded a couple bends when, to his surprise, he saw Owl Man not far behind him. No wonder everyone thought him so wise. He had slipped behind and watched for Blue Jay so he would know exactly where he was. In doing this, Blue Jay led Owl Man straight to the short-cut. Poor Frog Boy was leaping over logs and hopping over brush on the long trail behind Bear.

Owl Man and Blue Jay were racing close to each other now. A glimpse of these two racing through the timber, avoiding trees and stones, was a wondrous thing to see. Owl Man could move so silently but Blue Jay was fun and exciting to watch.

When they came within site of the village, Blue Jay realized he could not beat Owl Man in a direct race for the victory.

So he called over to Owl Man "Wait my cousin! We must stop and plan our entry so there is no doubt about the winner."

Owl Man smiled, as he was pretty sure Blue Jay wanted to rest so they looked more fresh and handsome as they entered the village.

"How about over here in the shade" asked Owl Man?

"I have a need to share my heart thoughts with you Owl Man," said Blue Jay. He was straightening the black moss on his legs so he could look even more powerful as he entered the village.

"Owl Man, I have great respect for you. You have been honest and honorable in this race" humbly stated Blue Jay.

"Thank you little cousin, I am not called wise because I do foolish things. But I would never try to cheat my brothers by trickery like our silly cousin Coyote" replied Owl Man.

Blue Jay bent his head down ashamed and sat on a huge rock near Owl Man. "You have seen through my plan to win Princess Jay haven't you?" asked Blue Jay.

"Yes I have and I know you were not alone in your plan. I heard Princess Jay tell you how to win the race," said Owl Man with a very knowing look.

"I am ashamed to have been so unfair to you Owl Man, but her father would never hear my request for Princess Jay and we love each other," said Blue Jay with his head falling even farther.

"Whooo do you think understands?" asked Owl Man. "I have a wise, strong, and beautiful mate at my home tribe. I came to make sure someone of good humor and strength would one day replace Selfish as my neighbor," he said.

"Now I am confused," said Blue Jay "Why would you want two wives?"

"I do not," said Owl Man. "I only wanted to help the right person win and since I can see your love for Princess Jay is returned by her and that you are much more joyful and kind than Selfish, I came to help you win this contest."

With a jump for joy, Blue Jay said, "Then let us finish this race and make our people happy!"

"Go, my little cousin, and I will follow," said Owl Man.

With that, Blue Jay simply danced the last few yards to the finish line and, being the first to arrive, was met with cheers, yells, and songs by all in the tribe. At the appearance of Blue Jay and not Bear, Selfish began to quiet the crowd and say "Wait, Wait my people, this one has cheated. He is not the best nor the strongest of these men."

Owl Man came to the finish line next and then Bear followed by Frog Boy and all the others who had run the race. They realized that old Selfish was about to stop the wedding feast and not let Blue Jay claim his mate. They all began saying at once, "No this one came in first! This one is the best of us! This one is the smartest! This one is the winner!"

Again, Selfish tried to complain, but Owl Man came forward and said, "It is your daughter who set the terms of this race. It is up to her to say whooo is the winner."

All the tribe agreed and Selfish could do nothing to prevent Princess Jay from declaring the winner. Princess Jay had been to her secret tree, meeting place to offer a prayer for Blue Jay, when she found the bundle of Sacred Stones that Blue Jay had gathered. All day she had been trying to figure out how to get them to him before the race ended. Now it looked as if there was a chance.

"Did you gather all the gifts I requested for my People?" she asked as she bent near him and slipped him the bundle of sacred items.

"Yes and I have many good racers to thank for these

gifts as they all helped in their gathering" Blue Jay answered. No one knew what he meant by these words but they were spoken honorably and humbly so they cheered again and some hit the drum with a joyful rhythm.

First he took out the most beautiful piece of sacred Pipe Stone the people had ever seen. That is all the people but Selfish. He knew it was the very piece he had cheated Owl Man out of last summer and the one he had loaned to Bear to win this contest. He did not say anything for fear he would give away his plot for Bear to win. But Selfish could hardly contain his anger. What had that dumb Bear done?

"Here also is a sacred healing Crystal from the waters of Healing River," he said as he bent forward to hand the beautiful stone to Princess Jay.

This time Selfish drew his breath in so quickly he choked and sputtered out "That cannot be the one you found this day. You stole that stone from me. I was gifted it by my good friend Bear last winter. Isn't that right Bear?"

"Oh no, my Chief, that is the one you stole from me last winter, and then gave it to me this morning so I could win the race. But I have given it to Blue Jay because he is the best man for your daughter. I do not want to be Chief," answered Bear.

Everyone laughed as they saw the look that Selfish gave Bear.

Blue Jay then handed Princess Jay the most fragrant and wonderful Sweet Grass Braids she had ever seen. "These" he said "I have gathered from Sweet Grass Meadow this very day to show you how full my heart is with love for you Princess Jay" and he bowed his head with a slight blush on his dark cheeks.

As Princess Jay stepped forward, Blue Jay was fluffing out the moss on his legs to make himself look stronger than all the others. She smiled and told all who could hear her voice.

"This is Blue Jay and he has won the race. He is the

strongest of all these young men and the wisest to humbly honor his brothers for their gifts. As we have seen, my father has been a selfish leader. I give you, my people, a new Chief this day for Blue Jay will be my mate," cried out Princess Jay.

Selfish could only moan from his pile of furs and pelts as his fat wife brought him fry bread to ease his pain.

With that, Blue Jay swept Princess Jay up in his arms and, as he waded across the river to the wedding feast, all the moss got wet and fell off his legs. Everyone laughed and was happy and excited about having a chief who was so funny. For as the moss washed down the river, everyone could see that Blue Jay had long skinny legs with no muscles at all!

Now you know how Blue Jay won his bride! The beautiful and silly cousin of Magpie and Crow is very handsome in his fine blue feathers, but he still to this very day, has skinny legs!

White Buffalo Calf Woman

This legend has a long and deep history among many Native tribes but is credited to the Buffalo Tribes of the Sioux Nation. To many Native Americans, Buffalo is more than the animal that supplies food, garments, and tools. Buffalo was and is a center focal point in many spiritual beliefs and ceremonial offerings. This legend has many layers to it and was told with as much detail as time allowed. The story told here is how I remember hearing it when I was young.

I do not remember who told it the first time I really listened, as it has been given voice by many elders, relatives, and friends over the years. The various versions of this legend are each beautiful in their own right. The lessons are always the same if we pay attention, but the way the message is wrapped in the words of the storyteller will be slightly different. I share these with you from my voice with the hope that you enjoy it as much as I do.

On a day, like any other, when everything was different, two young men from the tribe went looking for a Buffalo heard. They were cousins who had grown up together in the traditional ways of their people. Best friends and battling buddies who could practice for manhood through competition and games. If they could locate a Buffalo herd they would return to the tribe feeling blessed by Creator and proud of their skills. A hunting party would be gathered and they could be allowed to lead it. This was a great honor for two young men, not yet grown. They would feel pride in the respect they could earn this day, if they were successful. It is good to have self-confidence for all men and women of every age. Taking pride in ones accomplishments is not walking the edge of ego, but rather is an expression of a healthy relationship with the Spirit inside every two-legged.

As they came to the top of a ridge they saw a herd of Buffalo feeding not far off. They used great hunting skills and crawled on their bellies to a place where they could better see the herd. As they rose up, on bent elbows, to look at the herd they were shocked to see instead, a beautiful young maiden.

She was dressed in pure white doe skin. Her long black hair was free and unbraided. It hung from the most beautifully beaded headband. An Eagle feather of great age and value draped one side of her face. The fringe on her outfit was so long, it looked as if she was clothed in a white waterfall. The breeze blew her hair and the fringe in a gentle hypnotic sway.

Turquoise necklaces, crafted of the finest silver, glinted in the sun light, from their resting place on her elegant neck. She smiled softly at the young men. Her dark brown eyes were glowing from sun kissed skin. Her lips were full and colored with sweet-cherry juice, stain. Her tiny feet were barely visible in their finely beaded moccasins, as the peeked from under the long fringe of her gown.

She was a woman like none these young ones had ever seen. Her beauty was enhanced by the cleansing smell of sage that blew across the faces of the young men. The Buffalo herd was still as death watching the maiden where she stood, looking at the young ones.

In only a moment, or maybe an hour, the first young man spoke from his selfish man place whispering to his cousin he said "No other two-legged is near-by; no one can see us. Ay let us take this beautiful woman for our pleasure. We can lay with her here in the grass and enjoy this day".

His cousin grabbed his arm and said, "No, we need to honor this one. She is Sacred and has much to teach us" for his heart was touched by her spirit.

The first young man ignored the good and wise council of his cousin. He ran down the hillside, with his feet slipping on the tall sweet grass. He was determined to capture the maiden. She did not show fear or try to escape, but rather extended her arms wide, as if to embrace him. He let out a whoop of joy and ran into her arms. Suddenly a great cloud of dust surrounded them and they were visible to no man.

The wind was not blowing on the tall sweet grass. The breeze could not be felt on the cousin's cheek. But around the maiden a whirlwind of dust blew so strong that the funnel rose up to the center of Cloud People's Nation.

When the dust came to earth and rested at the feet of the maiden, the first young man's bones lie dried and dead on the ground. Not one hair on her head was out of place, no fringe was cast aside. She stood in her perfection as they had first seen her.

Fear struck the heart of the remaining youth and he bent to the ground with head lowered. He asked Wakhan Tunkasila to protect him from this spirit woman. For he could see his dead cousin's bones glowing white at her feet.

Creator spoke to his heart, not with words for his ears, but with an unmistakable message "Be brave, have no fear, this Spirit is from me. I send her with a gift for you and your people."

The young hunter stood up and as he felt beckoned, walked slowly toward the beautiful maiden, with knees shaking. His eyes lowered to the ground and he spoke with the quivering voice of a child.

"If you wish food and drink I am happy to invite you to my village" he managed to say barely aloud.

She said nothing but only looked through his heart. He feared his voice was too timid so he spoke again only slightly, more steady, "My mother and father would be honored to offer you protection, if you wish to visit my village."

He knew in his heart that she had many lessons to teach the people of his tribe. So he tried once more to invite her to follow him home. "You are welcome to come rest in the hospitality of my families lodge, only follow my steps if you wish to come."

And he turned slowly to walk up the hill while looking over his shoulder at the beautiful woman.

But she said, in a voice sounding like night owl's song, "I will not visit your village this day." But she motioned him to come close saying she had for him a gift. With fear in his heart and trembling in his hands, he went to her.

She said, "Because you come humbly and honorably to me, I will give you this great gift for your people."

As she stretched out her hand in welcome to him he began to feel less fear and noticed a warm calm settle on his heart.

She said, "I am the one called White Buffalo Calf Woman and I carry a Sacred Pipe for smoking the herbs of this land. When your people blow smoke from this pipe out of their mouth, your sister Wind will gather it. She will take it to rest on mighty Eagles wing, as he can lift it to the above home of our Great Spirit. He will see the people's prayers on their breath of sacred smoke. He will answer quickly the needs of the people." She handed him a pipe bowl made from a beautiful red stone and a pipe stem made of cedar wood.

He asked her how to use this great gift, but she would

only say to return to his people and prepare for her visit. Then another mighty dust cloud consumed the maiden and when it had cleared, all the youth could see was a small white Buffalo calf walking into the herd of many Buffalo.

When the frightened young hunter returned to his village alone, with only the pipe and not his cousin, the elders took him to their private council lodge and began to question him. There was a light in his eyes saying he had been touched by Spirit.

He told them of all that he had seen and felt on this day. He stated how in his confusion he was not sure if these things were real or a vision. The elders were very wise and told the young man that he would be called Pipe Carrier from this day on and that if it were a true vision; he would learn soon how to receive this wonderful gift.

Four days later from the West, the place of dreams and night resting, came a young and beautiful maiden to the village. All the people could see her walking in a cloud of dust, with her white leather fringe flowing about her. As she came near, she called for Pipe Carrier to come and escort her to the elders lodge.

He came forward with his head lowered in respect. He noticed her slight smile and how she looked into his heart and not only his eyes. As he approached her, he lifted the pipe in both upturned palms, to offer it in a respectful manner.

She took the pipe from Pipe Carrier and said, "I have many things to share with you and your people on this day. I hope your ears are open and your heart is willing to listen."

She honored him for his pure heart and said, "Because you did not looked on me in a disrespectful manner, but rather recognized the Spirit that moves through me, I am willing to share these great wisdoms with you."

Pipe Carrier realized he had been protected by his innocent manner and his fear. When one is trained to always be brave, it can be worrisome to feel fear. He was not aware of how fear is also a great teacher and protector of the two-legged. Many things of the heart are not recognized by the mind and can create confusion in the thoughts. Pipe Carrier knew he was going to live his life in a way that would honor the pipe and this Spirit Woman.

The first tradition of the pipe she taught the people was about the significance of Wakhan Chanupa (Sacred Pipe). She spoke of a need for the people of all lands to greet each other with peaceful intentions and hospitality. She explained how the pipe could open the blessings of clear communication. It would unite the people of many tribes. This symbol of peace would teach the generations from now on until all eternity is fulfilled.

As she spoke to the people she held the pipe, wrapped in its leather bag, tenderly in her arms as if it were an infant. She spoke to Pipe Carrier while his tribal members looked on.

Then the beautiful maiden looked to Pipe Carrier who understood without her speaking a word. He reached for the wool blanket wrapped around his shoulders and taking it from his body; he spread it on the ground before her feet. She gracefully knelt with her knees on the blanket. She pulled from her belt a length of red wool and spread it on the blanket in front of her. She laid the pipe, wrapped in its leather bag, carefully on the wool.

She leaned forward and looked at a twig of sage on a near-by bush. By some form of magic it came to her hand and smoldered its curl of fine, sweet, smoke around her hands and face. While she smudged herself the tribal members sat on the ground in a circle around her so they could witness her motions and understand her words. When the smudge was complete the sage evaporated into the air and left her hands free to address the pipe.

Pipe Carrier jumper up and ran to his lodge where he had a bundle of sage with a feather fan and an abalone shell. When he returned he carefully placed it on the blanket, within reach of the maiden. She removed two bundles from the pipe bag, each wrapped in red wool.

She opened the first bundle and held in her hands a beautiful stone pipe bowl. She spoke softly as she held the bowl for all to see.

"The bowl of this pipe represents the womb of the women of your tribe. It holds the gift of birth and life connection with Creator. The offerings and prayers made with this bowl will give each one who participates, the ability to give birth to new thoughts, new ideas, new courage, and new connection. Just as the child is born innocent and in harmony with all Mytakwe Oyasin, the ones who share the pipe will also be in harmony," she said.

"The stem of the pipe represents the child making part of your men. The strength and endurance of Cedar tree is held in the wood of this stem. It is a reminder of the gifts our men can offer the tribe as good providers and protectors of all. It is also a reminder that they must not be overly aggressive or they can be broken. They must realize that only Creator plants the seeds that give life. The men who walk in honor and humility before the Creator are always the most respected of our tribe," she continued.

As she spoke these words, she un-wrapped a smooth cedar pipe stem, covered with beaded dressings and leather fringe. The craftsmanship was wondrous to see. A hushed, collective breath of "aahhh" came from the on-lookers.

The maiden now held both pieces in her hands and with palms open she let them be seen by all. She spoke with gentleness and strength as if addressing her most cherished child.

"These two parts should be kept separate except at times of ceremony. The bowl should be wrapped in its red cloth or leather and the stem wrapped in a separate piece of red cloth or leather. Then both wrapped pieces can be placed in a pipe bag made of leather or wool, like this one" she said.

"Today I will open this Wakhan Chanupa (Sacred

Pipe) for you to share." It will guide your prayer thoughts and help you ask for the guidance you need. It can empower your prayers of gratitude to bless our Creator," she said.

Her hands moved to bring the two pieces together and as she spoke, the stem and the bowl were joined.

"When they come together, they give birth to our prayers," she said.

She reached into an unseen bag from around her waist and took out a small leather pouch. She again held the pipe across one arm as if it were a small infant.

She began to explain, "In this pouch is the sacred herb of Tobacco. It is the herb of unity. It brings your cousins from other lands to trade for the good Buffalo meat you preserve. When those of the Salmon tribes and those of the Buffalo tribes meet, they can share Wakhan Chanupa before the Good Trade is made."

She continued, "When sacred herb mixtures are placed in the bowl of this pipe and fire from the red coals is held near, there will be smoke. It will appear as my dust, and the people will breathe it in. When the people blow out this sacred smoke, we of the spirit world will see the prayers of their breath. When we watch this breath float to the sky nation, we will know your needs and we will accept your praise and gratitude. You will be given many ceremonies and taught sacred words for this purpose."

"The first of these ceremonies will be to honor the four directions. You have come to be a ceremony from the great womb of Mother Earth. It is your duty to return honor to her. Set upon the ground four stones, one for each direction, that is North, South, East, and West. Place a larger stone in the center of this sacred circle for an altar to the Great Creator and a smaller stone beside it for Mother Earth," she said.

"Take the leaves from the tobacco plant and crush them. You will learn other smoking mixtures from vision and dreams but for this thanksgiving ceremony, you need only tobacco. Give a pinch of the tobacco to the pipe while facing East and say words of this fashion, 'honor is given to East, for the birth of Sun each morning', Then drop a pinch of tobacco on the rock at the East corner of the circle" she said.

"Turn to face the South rock and again place a pinch of the tobacco in the pipe and this time speak something like these words, 'To South I give praise for it is the place of our ancestors and the growth of wisdom' then to the rock of the South corner give a pinch of tobacco" she demonstrated as she spoke.

"Now look to the stone in West and place a pinch of sacred tobacco in the pipe and say, 'Thank you and honor to West for the dark place of dreams, visions and rest. Then give tobacco to the West stone," she said as her hands gracefully dropped bits of tobacco on the stone.

"Turn to the North and as you fill the balance of the pipe with sacred tobacco say, 'North, place of the freeze and snow that kills disease and brings water and purity I honor you' and again give the stone of this corner the gift of tobacco" she said.

Then she said, "Step back to the center of the circle and on bended knee, give tobacco to Mother Earth as you tell her "Thank you for giving Mytakwe Oyasin life".

"Now you can stand before your Creator and with head lifted to the sky you can offer Wakhan Tunkasila a gift of tobacco to be carried by the breeze and say to Him, 'The color of blue has been given to us as a reminder of your Sky Nation. We know that all life is a gift from you and in your creation we live only to honor you. Please accept our prayers, as humbly we come to bow before your mighty strength" she spoke the powerful words with humble respect.

"Now you can light the pipe and blow your prayer breaths to the four directions. You can say any honorable thing in your heart to the directions and know that the Spirits can see your breath. We will carry these prayers on the winds, with the help of Winged Ones, to the Great Mystery and you will know we are with you," she continued.

"This is the Pipe Ceremony that can open your heart and your mind to the wonders of Great Spirit. You will receive many other ceremonies but first you will learn to speak in this honorable way to your Creator. These words are not to be memorized and used as the song of a child, for they will come from your heart in this manner and will bring you to remember your Creator. The gift of Pipe is Sacred and you must use it in an honorable way. Remember the young warrior consumed by his own selfishness and do not abuse this gift" she said.

That was the first lesson in Pipe Ceremony brought to our people by White Buffalo Calf Woman.

Made in the USA
Middletown, DE
24 February 2024